Enchanted Yule

Enchanted Yule

Matthew Petchinsky

Enchanted Yule: A Wiccan and Pagan Guide to a Magical and Memorable Season

By : Matthew Petchinsky

Introduction

Welcome to the Season of Yule: Embracing the Old Ways for Modern Joy

As the wheel of the year turns, the season of Yule beckons us with its serene beauty, sacred energy, and ancient traditions. Yule, celebrated at the Winter Solstice, marks the longest night and the rebirth of the Sun, symbolizing hope, renewal, and the promise of brighter days ahead. Rooted in pagan and earth-based spirituality, this festival predates many modern winter celebrations, offering us a glimpse into a time when humanity lived in harmony with the natural cycles of the Earth.

This guide invites you to reconnect with the magic of Yule, honoring its ancient customs while adapting them to enrich your modern life. Whether you are new to pagan traditions or a seasoned practitioner, this journey through Yule will inspire you to embrace the old ways with renewed purpose, weaving them seamlessly into your personal and communal celebrations.

In a world often marked by chaos and haste, Yule serves as a reminder to pause, reflect, and celebrate the enduring rhythm of life. From decorating with evergreens to lighting candles in honor of the returning Sun, every act performed during this season carries the weight of generations past and the promise of hope for the future. By embracing the essence of Yule, you not only nurture your spirit but also cultivate joy, connection, and a profound sense of belonging.

The Spirit of Yule: Origins, Traditions, and the Sacred Energy of the Winter Solstice

Yule's origins lie in the ancient pagan and Norse traditions of Northern Europe, where communities gathered to honor the Winter Solstice. Known as *Jul* to the Norse and *Giuli* to the Anglo-Saxons, this festival celebrated the Sun's rebirth after the darkest night of the year. Fires were lit, feasts were shared, and offerings were made to deities and spirits to ensure protection, prosperity, and the return of fertile lands in the coming year.

Central to the Yule celebration is the Yule log, a symbol of warmth, light, and protection. In early practices, a great log was brought into the home, blessed, and burned in the hearth, its flames representing the rekindling of the Sun's strength. Today, the Yule log endures as a cherished tradition, often recreated as a cake or candle display, embodying the continuity of light and life.

Evergreens—holly, ivy, pine, and mistletoe—are another vital aspect of Yule. These plants, thriving even in the heart of winter, symbolize resilience, vitality, and eternal life. Decorating with evergreens not only brings nature indoors but also serves as a living connection to the divine energies of the season.

The Winter Solstice itself is a potent time for reflection, introspection, and spiritual renewal. As the Sun pauses at its southernmost point before beginning its journey northward, we too are encouraged to pause, assess the past, and set intentions for the future. Yule is a time to honor the duality of darkness and light within ourselves and the world, finding harmony in the balance they create.

Modern Yule celebrations often intertwine with other holiday traditions, such as Christmas, reflecting the syncretic evolution of cultural practices over centuries. Yet, at its core, Yule remains a deeply spiritual and personal festival. It invites us to honor the cycles of the Earth, our ancestors, and the divine forces that guide us.

This book is a journey through the heart of Yule. It will guide you through its rich history, sacred rituals, and creative ways to celebrate this season with authenticity and joy. Whether you are lighting candles in solitude, gathering around a fire with loved ones, or crafting your own Yule decorations, may this guide empower you to forge a deeper connection with the magic of the Winter Solstice.

As you turn the pages, allow the wisdom of the old ways to inspire your spirit and enrich your celebrations. Yule is not merely a festival—it is a timeless expression of humanity's enduring relationship with the natural world. Welcome to the season of Yule, a time to honor the past, embrace the present, and celebrate the promise of brighter days to come.

Chapter 1: The Magic of Preparation

The season of Yule begins not with the lighting of candles or the sharing of feasts, but with the mindful preparation of your space and spirit. Preparation is an act of magic in itself, infusing your environment with intention and creating a foundation for the sacred energy of the Winter Solstice. Through the acts of cleansing, blessing, and intentional decoration, you align your surroundings with the spirit of Yule, inviting warmth, renewal, and the blessings of the season into your life.

Cleansing and Blessing Your Space for Yule Celebrations

Before any celebration begins, it is essential to cleanse your space of residual energy and create a blank canvas for new, vibrant energy to flow. Yule is a time of transition and rebirth, and by purifying your environment, you set the stage for welcoming the light of the returning Sun.

1. Physical Cleansing

Start by physically tidying your space. Dust surfaces, sweep floors, and declutter areas that have accumulated unnecessary items. Focus particularly on the hearth, as it symbolizes warmth, protection, and the rebirth of light during Yule. If you do not have a hearth, designate a central area in your home to serve as your sacred focal point.

As you clean, visualize sweeping away stagnant energy along with the physical dust. Imagine your space becoming lighter, brighter, and more welcoming with every action.

2. Energetic Cleansing

Once your space is physically clean, it's time to cleanse it energetically. Choose a cleansing method that resonates with your practice:

- **Smudging:** Use dried herbs like sage, cedar, or rosemary, traditionally associated with purification and protection. Light the bundle, allow it to smolder, and waft the smoke around the room, focusing on corners, doorways, and windows.
- **Sound Cleansing:** Ring a bell, use a singing bowl, or play harmonious music to disperse negative energy and invite in uplifting vibrations.
- **Sprinkling or Spraying:** Create a cleansing spray using moon water or water infused with essential oils like lavender, pine, or frankincense, and lightly mist your space.

As you cleanse, repeat a blessing or affirmation, such as:
"I cleanse this space of all that no longer serves and welcome the light and joy of Yule into my home."

3. Blessing Your Space

After cleansing, bless your space to align it with the energies of Yule. Place your hands on walls, doorways, and furniture, and visualize them glowing with warm, golden light. You may also use a blessing oil—such as one made from cinnamon, orange, and clove—to anoint doorframes, windowsills, and your altar.

Recite an invocation, such as:
"May this home be blessed with peace, love, and prosperity this Yule season. May it be a sanctuary of warmth, joy, and renewal for all who dwell here."

Creating Sacred Energy through Intentional Decoration

Once your space is cleansed and blessed, it's time to transform it into a sacred environment that reflects the magic of Yule. Decorations are not merely aesthetic—they are powerful symbols that carry spiritual meaning and amplify your intentions.

1. Evergreen Adornments

Evergreens like pine, cedar, holly, and ivy are central to Yule decorations, representing resilience, protection, and eternal life. Use these natural elements to adorn your home:

- Create a Yule wreath for your front door to invite protection and blessings.
- Drape garlands of evergreen across mantels, staircases, and windows.
- Place sprigs of holly and ivy on your altar to honor the balance of light and dark.

For added intention, bless your evergreens by sprinkling them with salt water or smudging them with smoke before placing them in your home.

2. Candles and Lighting

Light plays a vital role in Yule, symbolizing the return of the Sun. Incorporate candles, lanterns, and string lights to create a warm, inviting atmosphere. Choose colors like gold, red, green, and white to align with the season's energy.

- Arrange candles in a circle on your altar to represent the wheel of the year.

- Place a large central candle—your "Yule Candle"—to symbolize the rebirth of light.

As you light your candles, set an intention:
"As this flame grows, so does the light within me and around me. May it guide my path and illuminate the way forward."

3. Yule Altar

Create or refresh your altar for Yule with items that resonate with the season:

- **Natural Elements:** Pinecones, acorns, and dried fruits symbolize abundance and fertility.
- **Crystals:** Stones like citrine, garnet, and clear quartz amplify the energy of renewal, prosperity, and clarity.
- **Symbols of the Sun:** Add sun-shaped ornaments, gold coins, or solar imagery to honor the returning light.

Arrange these items mindfully, allowing your altar to serve as a focal point for your celebrations and meditations.

4. Personal Touches

Infuse your decorations with personal meaning by including handmade items, family heirlooms, or items that reflect your unique connection to Yule. Create ornaments, garlands, or centerpieces using natural materials like dried oranges, cinnamon sticks, and cloves, which also fill your space with the comforting scents of the season.

5. The Yule Log

The Yule log is one of the most iconic symbols of the season. If you have a fireplace, select a log from an oak, birch, or ash tree, decorate it with ribbons and sprigs of holly, and burn it during your celebrations.

For modern homes without fireplaces, craft a decorative Yule log by arranging three candles (representing the past, present, and future) on a wooden base adorned with greenery and seasonal symbols. Light the candles as part of your Solstice rituals.

The Intentional Magic of Preparation

The process of preparing your space for Yule is more than a series of tasks—it is a sacred ritual in its own right. Each action, from cleansing to decorating, holds the power to transform your home into a sanctuary of warmth and magic. By approaching these preparations with mindfulness and intention, you align yourself with the spirit of the season, creating a harmonious and sacred space where the light of Yule can shine brightly.

Through this act of preparation, you honor the ancient traditions of your ancestors while infusing your celebrations with modern joy. As you move forward into the heart of Yule, let the energy of your prepared space support and uplift you, reminding you of the magic that lives in both the season and your spirit.

Chapter 2: Yule Altars and Ritual Spaces

A Yule altar is the heart of your Winter Solstice celebrations—a sacred space that embodies your spiritual intentions and honors the Sun's return. Whether you have a dedicated altar year-round or are creating one specifically for Yule, this chapter will guide you through designing an altar that aligns with the season's energies. By incorporating seasonal symbols and personal touches, your altar becomes a focal point for your rituals, meditations, and celebrations, radiating warmth, renewal, and sacred energy.

Designing a Yule Altar to Honor the Sun's Return

The Winter Solstice, or Yule, celebrates the rebirth of the Sun after the longest night of the year. Your Yule altar should reflect this theme of renewal, light, and the enduring cycle of life. To begin, select a location that feels sacred and peaceful—a corner of your home, a tabletop, or even an outdoor space can serve as your altar.

1. Choosing the Foundation

The foundation of your altar sets the tone for your Yule celebrations. Use a cloth or covering that resonates with the season's colors and themes:

- **Gold and Yellow:** Represent the returning Sun and its vibrant energy.
- **Red and Green:** Symbolize life, vitality, and the evergreen nature of the spirit.
- **White and Silver:** Reflect the purity of snow and the moon's guidance through the dark night.

You may also use natural materials like burlap, woven fabric, or sheepskin to ground your altar in an earth-centered aesthetic.

2. Setting the Layout

The layout of your altar can follow traditional patterns or reflect your personal creativity. Consider these symbolic arrangements:

- **Circular Layout:** Representing the cyclical nature of the year, with candles, crystals, and symbols arranged in a ring.
- **Solar Focus:** Place a central candle or Sun symbol in the middle of your altar, surrounded by other elements to draw attention to the theme of renewal.
- **Directional Correspondence:** Align your altar with the cardinal directions, incorporating elements that correspond to Earth (North), Air (East), Fire (South), and Water (West).

3. Incorporating the Sun

Since Yule celebrates the Sun's rebirth, include items that honor its return:

- A golden or yellow candle to represent the Sun's light.
- Sun-shaped ornaments or carvings.
- Citrine, sunstone, or amber crystals for their solar energy.

When lighting the Sun candle on your altar, focus your intention on welcoming warmth and light into your life and your home.

Enhancing Spiritual Energy with Seasonal Symbols

Symbols carry deep spiritual significance, and by incorporating them into your altar, you amplify the energy of Yule and align yourself with its themes of hope, renewal, and abundance. Each symbol you choose represents an aspect of the season's magic, offering opportunities for meditation, ritual, and connection.

1. Evergreen Elements

Evergreens are central to Yule celebrations, symbolizing eternal life and resilience. Incorporate sprigs of holly, ivy, pine, cedar, or juniper onto your altar. These plants also serve as offerings to deities, spirits, or ancestors.

- **Holly:** Represents protection and the balance of masculine and feminine energies.
- **Ivy:** Symbolizes interconnectedness and the cycles of life.
- **Pinecones:** Represent fertility and the seeds of new beginnings.

2. Crystals and Stones

Crystals resonate with the energy of Yule, enhancing the spiritual vibrations of your space. Place them around your altar or use them in rituals:

- **Clear Quartz:** Amplifies intentions and brings clarity.
- **Citrine:** Enhances joy, abundance, and solar energy.
- **Garnet:** Promotes strength, vitality, and grounding.

Cleanse and charge your crystals by placing them under the light of the Solstice Sun or the Full Moon before adding them to your altar.

3. Candles and Lighting

Light is a powerful symbol of Yule, representing the Sun's rebirth and the illumination of the spirit. Use candles in your altar design to enhance this energy.

- **Yule Candle:** A large central candle in gold, yellow, or red serves as the Sun's symbolic representation.
- **Color-Theme Candles:** Arrange candles in seasonal colors like red, green, gold, and white.
- **Candle Magic:** Carve symbols or intentions into the wax of your candles for added potency.

As you light your candles, reflect on the return of light in both the natural world and your inner life. Recite a blessing, such as:
"With this flame, I welcome the Sun's return, bringing warmth, light, and renewal to my life and the world."

4. Offerings and Seasonal Items

Offerings honor the energies of the season and invite blessings into your life. Add items to your altar that carry symbolic meaning:

- **Dried Oranges and Cinnamon Sticks:** Represent abundance, warmth, and solar energy.
- **Clove-Stuffed Apples or Oranges:** Symbolize prosperity and the sweetness of life.
- **Seasonal Treats:** Include baked goods, mulled wine, or cider as offerings to spirits or deities.

5. Symbols of Rebirth and Balance

In addition to honoring the Sun, Yule celebrates the balance of dark and light and the cycle of rebirth. Include:

- **Eggs or Seeds:** Representing fertility and potential.
- **Mirrors:** Symbolizing reflection and the transition from darkness to light.
- **Antlers or Horns:** Representing the Horned God or the spirit of nature's vitality.

Activating Your Altar

Once your altar is set, activate it with intention. Stand before it and take a few moments to center yourself. Light the central candle and say a blessing or prayer, focusing on the energy you wish to bring into your space and your life.

Use your altar as a sacred focal point throughout the Yule season for:

- **Meditation:** Sit before your altar and reflect on the themes of Yule, such as renewal, abundance, and balance.
- **Rituals:** Perform daily or weekly rituals, lighting candles, making offerings, or reciting affirmations.
- **Gratitude Practice:** Place a small bowl on your altar to collect written notes of gratitude throughout the season.

Creating a Living Connection

Your Yule altar is a living, evolving space. Throughout the season, you can add or rearrange items, adapting it to reflect your ongoing journey. By designing an altar that honors the Sun's return and enhancing its energy with meaningful symbols, you cultivate a deep connection to the sacred energies of Yule.

This practice not only enriches your spiritual experience but also grounds you in the timeless rhythm of nature, aligning your celebrations with the enduring magic of the Winter Solstice. Let your altar be a beacon of light and hope, guiding you through the darkest days of the year and into the warmth and renewal of the seasons ahead.

Chapter 3: Crafting Handmade Gifts

Yule is a season of giving, and what better way to embody the spirit of the season than by creating handmade gifts imbued with magic and intention? Handmade gifts are more than just physical objects—they are extensions of your energy, creativity, and love. When crafted with care and charged with magical intent, these gifts become sacred offerings, carrying blessings and personal power to those who receive them.

In this chapter, we will explore the art of creating magically charged, handmade gifts and techniques for infusing personal power and intent into every creation. Whether you are crafting for loved ones or creating offerings for deities or spirits, these gifts will reflect the magic of Yule and the warmth of your heart.

The Art of Creating Magically Charged, Handmade Gifts

The process of creating handmade gifts is inherently magical. By combining natural materials, creative energy, and spiritual intent, you can craft items that not only delight the recipient but also carry profound meaning and purpose.

1. Choosing Materials with Intention

The materials you select for your handmade gifts play a crucial role in their magical energy. Look for items that resonate with the themes of Yule—renewal, protection, abundance, and light. Some ideas include:

- **Natural Elements:** Wood, herbs, flowers, stones, and wax are grounding and connect your gifts to the earth's energy.
- **Colors of the Season:** Red, green, gold, white, and silver represent vitality, renewal, and the returning Sun.
- **Symbolic Inclusions:** Incorporate symbols like the Sun, stars, holly leaves, or spirals to enhance the gift's energy.

For example, a handmade candle infused with cinnamon and orange essential oils not only smells wonderful but also embodies the warmth and prosperity of Yule.

2. Creating Gifts with a Purpose

Every handmade gift can serve a specific purpose or intention. Consider what blessings you want to bestow upon the recipient:

- **Protection:** Create a charm or talisman using protective stones like black tourmaline or obsidian.
- **Abundance:** Craft a sachet filled with basil, bay leaves, and citrine to attract prosperity.
- **Healing and Comfort:** Knit a scarf or blanket, charging it with energy to soothe and nurture.

Each item you create should carry a specific intention that aligns with the recipient's needs or the spirit of the season.

3. Ritualizing the Crafting Process

Transform the act of crafting into a magical ritual by creating a sacred workspace and focusing your energy on your intention.

- Begin by cleansing your crafting area with sage, incense, or sound to remove any negative energy.
- Light a candle or play soft music to set the mood and connect with the spirit of Yule.
- As you work, recite affirmations or blessings, such as:
  "With every stitch, I weave love and protection. With every fold, I create warmth and joy. May this gift bring blessings to the one who receives it."

By approaching your crafting with mindfulness and intention, you infuse your gifts with powerful energy.

Infusing Personal Power and Intent into Every Gift

The true magic of handmade gifts lies in the personal power and intent you pour into them. This energy transforms ordinary objects into sacred talismans, carrying your love, care, and blessings to the recipient.

1. Charging Your Gifts with Energy

Before giving your handmade gifts, take a moment to charge them with your energy.

- Hold the gift in your hands and visualize it glowing with light, radiating warmth and love.
- Focus on the intention you want to embed within the gift—whether it's joy, protection, abundance, or healing.
- Say a blessing, such as:
  "I charge this gift with love, joy, and the magic of Yule. May it bring light and blessings to [recipient's name]."

If the gift is small, you can place it on your altar overnight, surrounded by candles or crystals, to further amplify its energy.

2. Personalizing the Gift with Symbols

Adding personal touches to your gifts strengthens their connection to the recipient. Consider incorporating symbols or elements that hold special meaning:

- Engrave or paint the recipient's initials or zodiac sign onto the gift.
- Include herbs or stones that align with the recipient's astrological sign or personal energy.
- Use symbols like runes, spirals, or pentacles to enhance the gift's spiritual power.

These details not only make the gift unique but also deepen its magical resonance.

3. Packaging with Intent

The way you package your gift can also carry magical intent. Use materials and colors that reflect your wishes for the recipient:

- Wrap the gift in natural fabrics like muslin or burlap to connect with earth energy.
- Add sprigs of holly, pine, or cinnamon sticks for seasonal blessings.
- Tie the package with red, gold, or green ribbons, visualizing the ribbon as a thread of protection or abundance.

You can also include a handwritten note or blessing card, detailing the intention behind the gift and offering guidance on how to use or appreciate it.

Handmade Gift Ideas for Yule

If you're unsure where to start, here are some ideas for handmade gifts that embody the spirit of Yule:

- **Spell Jars or Sachets:** Fill small jars or fabric pouches with herbs, crystals, and charms for protection, prosperity, or love.
- **Yule Candles:** Hand-pour candles scented with seasonal fragrances like cinnamon, clove, or pine.
- **Herbal Tea Blends:** Create a custom tea blend using dried herbs, such as chamomile, peppermint, and orange peel, for relaxation and renewal.
- **Wreaths or Garlands:** Craft decorative pieces using evergreen branches, pinecones, and ribbon.
- **Blessed Ornaments:** Paint or carve wooden ornaments and charge them with intentions for joy and harmony.
- **Baked Goods:** Infuse your holiday treats—cookies, breads, or spiced cakes—with love and gratitude as you prepare them.

Each of these gifts can be tailored to your recipient's needs and preferences, making them both meaningful and magical.

The Gift of Magic

Crafting handmade gifts is a deeply rewarding practice that connects you with the spirit of Yule. By pouring your energy, creativity, and intent into each creation, you transform the act of giving into a magical ritual. These gifts, infused with love and purpose, become powerful symbols of connection, gratitude, and renewal.

As you share your handmade creations, you not only honor the traditions of Yule but also spread its light and magic to those around you. Let this chapter inspire you to embrace the art of magical crafting, turning simple materials into treasures that carry the spirit of the season into the hearts of your loved ones.

Chapter 4: The Gift of Love

Yule is a time of connection—a season that invites us to deepen our bonds with family, friends, and loved ones while celebrating the light they bring into our lives. The spirit of Yule is not only about the gifts we exchange but also the love, gratitude, and care we infuse into every interaction. Through spells and rituals designed to strengthen relationships and thoughtful practices for expressing true love and appreciation, this chapter explores how to make the season a celebration of connection and heartfelt giving.

Spells and Rituals for Deepening Bonds with Family and Friends

During Yule, the long nights and cozy gatherings provide an ideal atmosphere for nurturing relationships. Spells and rituals can enhance these connections, creating a foundation of trust, love, and harmony that lasts beyond the season.

1. Family Harmony Ritual

Gathering with family during the holidays can sometimes bring up tension. This ritual fosters understanding, unity, and peace within the family.

- **Materials Needed:**
    - A white candle (for peace).
    - A green candle (for growth).
    - Lavender incense or essential oil (for calmness).
    - A small bowl of water (for emotional clarity).

Steps:

1. Set up a sacred space where the family can gather or where you can perform the ritual alone with the intention of spreading its effects to your family.
2. Light the candles and incense. Visualize a warm, golden light surrounding each family member, dissolving misunderstandings and creating harmony.
3. Dip your fingers into the water and sprinkle it lightly in the air, saying:
   "As the waters cleanse, so do our hearts clear. May peace flow freely among us here."
4. End by holding hands (if performing together) or placing your hands over your heart and sending gratitude to each family member.

2. Friendship Bonding Spell

This spell strengthens the bond between you and a friend, helping to foster deeper understanding and mutual support.

- **Materials Needed:**
  - Two small candles (one for each person, in colors representing your friendship).
  - A small piece of cord or ribbon (symbolizing connection).
  - A token of friendship (such as a charm or handwritten note).

Steps:

1. Light the candles and place them close together.
2. Tie the cord or ribbon loosely around the base of the candles, saying:

"By this knot, our bond is strong. Through all challenges, our friendship belongs."

3. Exchange the token with your friend, explaining its meaning and significance.

This spell works best when performed together, but it can also be done solo as an act of intention.

3. Love and Gratitude Ritual

This ritual is perfect for expressing love and gratitude to your closest relationships.

- **Materials Needed:**
  - A pink or red candle (for love).
  - Rose petals or rose oil.
  - A small journal or blank paper.

Steps:

1. Light the candle and sprinkle rose petals or anoint yourself with rose oil.
2. Write down one thing you love or appreciate about each person in your life. Be specific and heartfelt.
3. Hold the list close to your heart and say:
   "In this season of light, I honor the love in my life. May it grow stronger with each passing day."
4. Share your words with the people you've written about, either verbally or in a card or letter.

Expressing True Love and Gratitude in Gift-Giving

Gift-giving during Yule is not about material value but about the thought and love behind each offering. A truly meaningful gift carries the essence of your relationship, reflecting the unique connection you share with the recipient.

1. Thoughtful Selection

When choosing or creating a gift, consider the recipient's personality, needs, and interests. What would make them feel seen, appreciated, and loved? Some ideas include:

- A handmade item that reflects their hobbies or values.
- A book, journal, or tool that supports their growth or passions.
- A heartfelt letter expressing your love and gratitude.

The more personal and intentional the gift, the deeper its impact.

2. Personalizing Your Gifts

Adding a personal touch to your gifts enhances their emotional resonance. Some ideas for personalizing include:

- **Engraving or Monogramming:** Add the recipient's initials or a meaningful symbol.
- **Handwritten Notes:** Include a card or tag explaining why you chose the gift and what they mean to you.

- **Custom Elements:** Create something entirely unique, like a photo album, a scrapbook of memories, or a playlist of songs that remind you of them.

3. Infusing Gifts with Magic

Turn your gifts into talismans of love and gratitude by imbuing them with your personal energy:

- **Cleansing:** Use sage, incense, or moonlight to cleanse the gift before wrapping it.
- **Charging:** Hold the gift in your hands and visualize it glowing with the energy of your intention (love, protection, abundance, etc.).
- **Blessing:** Recite a simple spell or affirmation, such as:
  "May this gift carry joy and love. May it bring blessings from above."

4. Wrapping with Intention

The way you present your gift can add another layer of love and magic:

- Use seasonal colors and natural materials, like kraft paper, twine, or sprigs of evergreen.
- Incorporate symbols of Yule, such as stars, snowflakes, or holly.
- Include a small charm, such as a crystal or rune, tied to the ribbon as an added blessing.

The Magic of Love and Gratitude

The greatest gift you can offer during Yule is your presence and the genuine love you share with those around you. Spells and rituals help deepen your bonds, while thoughtful gift-giving becomes a physical expression of your care and gratitude.

Through the magic of love, Yule becomes more than a celebration of light—it becomes a celebration of the people who bring light into your life. As you connect with family and friends this season, let your actions, words, and gifts embody the true spirit of Yule: warmth, renewal, and unbreakable bonds.

Chapter 5: The Magic of Handmade Ornaments

Handmade ornaments are more than just decorations for the Yule season; they are tangible symbols of personal growth, abundance, and magical intent. Crafting ornaments allows you to channel your energy into a creative expression, turning simple materials into sacred objects that carry the essence of your intentions. Whether hung on a Yule tree, placed on an altar, or gifted to loved ones, these creations serve as reminders of your journey and the blessings you wish to attract.

This chapter explores how to craft ornaments that reflect your aspirations for personal growth and abundance and how to empower them with magical intent to infuse your holiday season with meaning and enchantment.

Crafting Ornaments to Represent Personal Growth and Abundance

Each ornament you create is an opportunity to manifest your intentions and reflect on your personal journey. By incorporating symbols and materials that resonate with growth and abundance, you create meaningful decorations that go beyond aesthetics.

1. Choosing Symbols of Growth and Abundance

When designing your ornaments, consider including symbols that represent your aspirations:

- **Tree of Life:** A powerful symbol of growth, connection, and the cycles of life.
- **Sun and Stars:** Represent illumination, guidance, and abundance.
- **Spirals:** Symbolize personal evolution and the journey toward self-fulfillment.
- **Acorns and Pinecones:** Represent potential, fertility, and prosperity.

These symbols can be painted, carved, or incorporated into the design of your ornaments.

2. Gathering Materials

The materials you use can enhance the energy of your creations. Opt for natural and meaningful items:

- **Wood or Clay:** Grounding materials that connect your creations to the Earth.
- **Crystals:** Small stones like citrine, garnet, or clear quartz can be embedded or tied to ornaments for their metaphysical properties.
- **Herbs and Spices:** Include sprigs of rosemary, cinnamon sticks, or dried orange slices for added symbolism and fragrance.
- **Ribbon and Twine:** Use colors like gold (abundance), green (growth), and red (passion and vitality).

3. Ornament Ideas for Personal Growth and Abundance

Here are some handmade ornament ideas that embody the spirit of Yule:

- **Intention Ornaments:** Write a specific goal or affirmation on a small piece of parchment, roll it up, and place it inside a clear ornament or hollow wooden bauble. Decorate the outside with symbols of success.
- **Rune-Adorned Ornaments:** Carve or paint runes such as *Fehu* (wealth) or *Algiz* (protection) onto wooden slices or clay disks.
- **Prosperity Stars:** Craft a star-shaped ornament using cinnamon sticks tied together with gold ribbon, and embellish it with dried herbs or crystals.
- **Sun Ornaments:** Create a golden Sun ornament out of polymer clay or papier-mâché, symbolizing the return of light and abundance.

- **Herbal Sachets:** Sew small fabric sachets filled with dried herbs like basil (prosperity) or lavender (calm), and hang them as ornaments.

4. Customizing with Personal Meaning

Add personal touches to your ornaments to make them uniquely yours:

- Include charms, initials, or birthstones that resonate with your identity.
- Incorporate elements from your environment, such as leaves, flowers, or feathers you've collected.
- Write dates or key milestones on the ornaments to commemorate important events from the past year.

Empowering Handmade Creations with Magical Intent

The magic of your ornaments lies in the energy and intention you pour into their creation. By consciously empowering them, you transform them into talismans that amplify your wishes and align with the spirit of Yule.

1. Setting Your Intention

Before you begin crafting, take a moment to reflect on the purpose of your ornaments. What do you want them to represent or attract?

- For growth, focus on themes like learning, resilience, or personal transformation.
- For abundance, center your intention on prosperity, opportunities, or gratitude.

Hold this intention in your mind as you work, allowing it to guide your choices and actions.

2. Creating in a Sacred Space

Transform your crafting area into a sacred workspace to enhance the energy of your creations:

- Cleanse the area with sage, incense, or sound before starting.
- Light a candle or play calming music to set a magical mood.
- Keep items like crystals, candles, or symbols of Yule nearby to inspire and energize your work.

3. Charging Your Ornaments with Energy

Once your ornaments are complete, empower them with your personal energy:

- Hold the ornament in your hands and visualize it glowing with the light of your intention. Imagine this light filling the ornament, sealing your wish inside.
- Speak an affirmation or blessing over the ornament, such as:
  "This ornament is a beacon of growth and abundance. May it carry my intention and manifest blessings in the year to come."

For an added boost, leave your ornaments on your altar overnight to absorb the energy of the season.

4. Using Correspondences for Added Power

Incorporate elements into your crafting process that correspond to your desired outcome:

- **Growth:** Use green materials, include spirals in your designs, and charge your ornaments under a waxing Moon.
- **Abundance:** Add gold accents, use herbs like basil or bay leaves, and charge your creations in the light of the Winter Solstice Sun.
- **Protection:** Use black or red ribbons, add protective runes, and charge your ornaments with obsidian or amethyst crystals.

5. Placing and Displaying Your Ornaments

Where and how you display your ornaments can enhance their magical impact:

- Hang them on your Yule tree to create a central hub of magical energy.
- Place them on your altar as part of your seasonal decorations.
- Use them as gifts, passing along their blessings to friends and family.

Each time you see or interact with the ornament, take a moment to reconnect with its intention, reinforcing its energy.

The Legacy of Handmade Ornaments

Crafting handmade ornaments is a magical practice that combines creativity, intention, and spiritual alignment. These decorations are more than seasonal embellishments—they are lasting symbols of your journey, your aspirations, and the blessings you wish to attract.

As you hang your ornaments on your tree, display them in your home, or gift them to loved ones, you create a legacy of love and magic that resonates far beyond the Yule season. Each handmade piece becomes a thread in the tapestry of your spiritual practice, reflecting the light and abundance you cultivate within yourself and share with the world.

Let the magic of handmade ornaments inspire you to embrace the season with creativity, mindfulness, and joy. Through their beauty and intent, these small creations carry the spirit of Yule into every corner of your life.

Chapter 6: Preparing a Feast

Yule is a time to gather with loved ones, celebrate the return of the Sun, and enjoy the bounty of the season. Central to this celebration is the Yule feast, a sacred and joyful event that combines traditional foods, seasonal ingredients, and magical intent. Preparing and sharing a meal at Yule nourishes not only the body but also the spirit, fostering connection, gratitude, and renewal.

This chapter explores the rich history of traditional Yule foods, provides recipes to inspire your Winter Solstice feast, and offers guidance on crafting seasonal dishes that align with the spirit of Yule.

Traditional Yule Foods: Recipes to Celebrate the Winter Solstice

Traditional Yule foods draw from ancient pagan customs and reflect the themes of abundance, warmth, and sustenance. These dishes often feature hearty, seasonal ingredients that embody the earth's gifts during the darkest time of the year

Wassail (Spiced Mulled Cider)

Wassail, a traditional Yule beverage, symbolizes prosperity and good health. This warm, spiced cider is perfect for toasting the season.

Ingredients:

- 1 gallon apple cider
- 2 cups orange juice
- ½ cup lemon juice
- 1 cup brown sugar
- 2 cinnamon sticks
- 1 tsp whole cloves
- 1 tsp allspice berries
- 1 orange, sliced
- Optional: 1 cup brandy (for an adult version)

Instructions:

1. Combine all ingredients in a large pot.
2. Simmer on low heat for 1–2 hours, stirring occasionally.
3. Strain the spices and serve warm in mugs.

Magical Intent: As you stir, focus on wishes for health, happiness, and abundance for the coming year.

Roast Pork with Apples and Herbs

Pork was often served at ancient Yule feasts as a symbol of prosperity and celebration. This recipe pairs savory roast pork with the sweetness of apples and herbs.

Ingredients:

- 1 boneless pork loin (about 3 lbs)
- 4 large apples, sliced
- 1 large onion, sliced
- 3 garlic cloves, minced
- 2 tbsp olive oil
- 2 tbsp fresh rosemary, chopped
- 2 tbsp fresh thyme, chopped
- Salt and pepper to taste

Instructions:

1. Preheat oven to 375°F (190°C).
2. Rub the pork loin with olive oil, garlic, rosemary, thyme, salt, and pepper.
3. Place the pork in a roasting pan and arrange apples and onions around it.
4. Roast for 1.5–2 hours, or until the internal temperature reaches 145°F (63°C).
5. Let the pork rest for 10 minutes before slicing and serving.

Magical Intent: Visualize abundance and stability as you prepare this dish, imagining it bringing prosperity to your household.

Winter Root Vegetable Soup

Root vegetables symbolize grounding and connection to the Earth, making them a perfect addition to your Yule feast.

Ingredients:

- 2 tbsp butter or olive oil
- 1 large onion, diced
- 2 garlic cloves, minced
- 3 carrots, peeled and diced
- 2 parsnips, peeled and diced
- 2 potatoes, peeled and diced
- 1 sweet potato, peeled and diced
- 6 cups vegetable stock
- 1 tsp dried thyme
- 1 tsp dried sage
- Salt and pepper to taste

Instructions:

1. Heat butter or oil in a large pot over medium heat. Sauté onion and garlic until fragrant.
2. Add the carrots, parsnips, potatoes, and sweet potato, cooking for 5–7 minutes.
3. Pour in the vegetable stock, thyme, and sage. Simmer for 20–30 minutes, or until vegetables are tender.
4. Blend part of the soup for a creamy texture, or leave it chunky. Season with salt and pepper.

Magical Intent: Focus on grounding and comfort as you chop the vegetables, envisioning the dish bringing warmth and stability to your loved ones.

Crafting Seasonal Dishes that Nourish Body and Spirit

The act of preparing a Yule feast is itself a magical ritual. Every ingredient, every stir of the pot, and every garnish can be imbued with intention. Crafting seasonal dishes allows you to connect with the rhythms of the Earth, honor ancient traditions, and infuse your celebrations with the energy of renewal.

1. Using Seasonal Ingredients

Winter's bounty may seem modest, but it offers rich flavors and hearty sustenance. Focus on these seasonal ingredients for your Yule feast:

- **Root Vegetables:** Carrots, potatoes, parsnips, and turnips symbolize grounding and resilience.
- **Apples and Pears:** Represent abundance, fertility, and sweetness.
- **Nuts and Seeds:** Embody potential and prosperity.
- **Herbs and Spices:** Use cinnamon, cloves, rosemary, and sage to add warmth and magical potency.

2. Cooking with Intention

Infuse your dishes with magical energy by incorporating your intentions into the preparation process:

- **Stirring:** Stir soups, sauces, or batter clockwise to attract positivity and abundance.
- **Blessing Ingredients:** Hold each ingredient in your hands and visualize it glowing with light before adding it to the dish.
- **Mindful Cooking:** Focus on love, gratitude, and joy as you cook, imagining these energies infusing the food.

3. Decorating the Table

Set your table with seasonal and magical elements to enhance the atmosphere:

- Use evergreen garlands, pinecones, and candles as a centerpiece.
- Include gold or red napkins and tableware to symbolize warmth and abundance.
- Place a small token of gratitude, such as a written blessing or charm, at each setting for guests to take home.

Sample Yule Feast Menu

For inspiration, here's a complete menu for a traditional Yule feast:

- **Appetizer:** Winter Root Vegetable Soup.
- **Main Course:** Roast Pork with Apples and Herbs, served with garlic mashed potatoes and roasted Brussels sprouts.
- **Side Dish:** Cranberry and walnut salad with a honey vinaigrette.
- **Dessert:** Gingerbread cake with whipped cream and spiced cookies.
- **Drink:** Wassail or mulled wine.

The Spirit of the Yule Feast

Preparing a feast for Yule is about more than just the food on the table—it's about the love, gratitude, and magic that go into every dish. By honoring the traditions of the Winter Solstice and incorporating your own intentions, you create a meal that nourishes both body and spirit.

As you sit down to enjoy your feast, take a moment to reflect on the blessings of the past year, the connections you share with those around you, and the light that is returning to the world. In this way, your Yule feast becomes a celebration of life, love, and the enduring cycles of the Earth.

Chapter 7: Celebrating with Nature

The season of Yule is deeply rooted in the cycles of nature, making it the perfect time to honor the Earth and connect with its rhythms. Celebrating outdoors or incorporating natural elements into your Yule practices strengthens your bond with the natural world, aligning your spirit with the energy of renewal, growth, and balance. This chapter explores how to host outdoor Yule rituals and incorporate nature into your celebrations, creating a harmonious connection between you, the Earth, and the cosmos.

Hosting Outdoor Yule Rituals: Honoring the Earth and Its Cycles

Outdoor rituals allow you to fully immerse yourself in the energy of the season. Whether under a crisp, starry sky or surrounded by snow-dusted trees, being in nature enhances your connection to the cycles of light and darkness, renewal, and growth.

1. Choosing a Sacred Location

Select a space that feels sacred and resonates with the spirit of Yule. This could be:

- A wooded area, symbolizing protection and grounding.
- A hilltop, offering a view of the horizon to watch the sunrise or sunset.
- A garden or backyard, where you can create a small ritual space.

Ensure the location is safe, accessible, and environmentally respectful.

2. Setting the Scene

Create an inviting and sacred outdoor space for your ritual:

- **Altar:** Set up a simple altar using a tree stump, rock, or portable table. Decorate it with candles, evergreen branches, pinecones, and other Yule symbols.

- **Circle of Light:** Arrange candles, lanterns, or solar lights in a circle to define the ritual area and symbolize the returning light.
- **Offerings:** Prepare biodegradable offerings, such as birdseed, flowers, or herbs, to give back to the Earth.

3. Outdoor Yule Ritual Ideas

- **Sunrise or Sunset Ceremony:**
    - Gather at dawn or dusk to honor the rebirth of the Sun.
    - Light a central candle or small bonfire as the Sun rises or sets, saying:
    "With this flame, we welcome the Sun's return. May its light bring warmth, renewal, and growth to the Earth and all living things."
    - Reflect on the cycles of light and darkness in your life and set intentions for the year ahead.
- **Earth Gratitude Ritual:**
    - Stand barefoot on the ground (if weather permits) or touch the Earth with your hands.
    - Offer thanks to the Earth for its gifts and blessings throughout the year.
    - Chant or recite:
    "Mother Earth, we honor you. Keeper of life, renewer of the soil, may our actions honor your sacred cycles."
- **Nature Walk and Offering:**
    - Take a meditative walk through a natural area, collecting small items like stones or fallen leaves to place on your altar.
    - Leave offerings of birdseed or herbs as an expression of gratitude to the land and its spirits.

4. Staying Comfortable and Safe

- Dress warmly in layers and bring blankets or hand warmers if the weather is cold.
- Keep candles or fires safely contained and have water or sand nearby for extinguishing.
- Be mindful of noise levels and leave no trace to respect the environment and others who may share the space.

Incorporating Nature into Your Yule Practices

If outdoor rituals aren't possible, you can still bring the magic of nature into your Yule celebrations. Incorporating natural elements into your home and practices fosters a deeper connection to the Earth and enhances the spiritual energy of the season.

1. Decorating with Natural Elements

Adorn your home with items sourced from nature to reflect the spirit of Yule:

- **Evergreens:** Use pine, cedar, or holly to create garlands, wreaths, or centerpieces.
- **Pinecones and Acorns:** Arrange them on your altar or use them as candle holders or ornaments.
- **Dried Fruits and Spices:** String dried orange slices, cinnamon sticks, and cranberries into garlands or use them to decorate your Yule tree.

As you decorate, bless the items with intentions for protection, abundance, and joy.

2. Crafting with Natural Materials

Create Yule crafts using materials from the Earth:

- **Nature Ornaments:** Make ornaments from twigs, berries, and pressed flowers.
- **Yule Logs:** Decorate a log with ribbons, greenery, and candles to serve as a centerpiece or symbolic offering.
- **Herbal Sachets:** Sew small sachets filled with dried herbs like rosemary, lavender, and sage to hang as ornaments or give as gifts.

3. Meditating with Nature

Even a simple moment spent in quiet reflection can deepen your connection to the Earth.

- Sit under a tree or by a window with a view of nature.
- Hold a stone, leaf, or piece of wood in your hands and focus on its texture, energy, and connection to the Earth.
- Reflect on the cycles of nature and how they mirror your own life's transitions.

4. Creating an Indoor Nature Altar

If you cannot celebrate outdoors, bring nature inside by creating an altar that honors the Earth's energy:

- Arrange stones, crystals, feathers, and natural items collected during walks.
- Add a bowl of water or soil to represent the Earth's life-giving forces.
- Include seasonal items like evergreen branches, pinecones, or candles to honor the season of Yule.

5. Giving Back to the Earth

Use Yule as an opportunity to express gratitude to the natural world and give back to the environment:

- Plant a tree or seeds as a symbol of growth and renewal.
- Create bird feeders using pinecones, peanut butter, and birdseed to support wildlife during winter.
- Commit to eco-friendly practices, such as reducing waste or using natural materials in your celebrations.

The Magic of Celebrating with Nature

Honoring nature during Yule is a profound way to connect with the rhythms of the Earth and the cosmos. Whether hosting an outdoor ritual or incorporating natural elements into your home, these practices deepen your spiritual experience and align you with the timeless cycles of light and darkness, death and rebirth.

Through these acts of celebration and reverence, you not only honor the season but also foster a sense of stewardship and gratitude for the Earth. As you celebrate with nature, may you find peace, renewal, and inspiration in its enduring beauty and wisdom.

Chapter 8: True Peace through Ritual

The holiday season, while joyous, can also bring stress, overcommitment, and emotional upheaval. Yule, however, offers an invitation to step back from the chaos and find true peace through intentional rituals. These practices help you cultivate inner harmony, align with the tranquil energy of the Winter Solstice, and center yourself amidst the busyness of the season.

In this chapter, we explore rituals designed to promote inner peace and harmony and provide techniques for aligning your energy with Yule's serene vibes, allowing you to embrace the season with a calm and open heart.

Rituals for Inner Peace and Harmony during the Holiday Season

Rituals for inner peace provide a sacred pause in the whirlwind of holiday preparations. These practices create space for reflection, grounding, and renewal, helping you navigate the season with grace and ease.

1. The Solstice Serenity Ritual

This ritual focuses on releasing tension and embracing the stillness of the Winter Solstice.

Materials Needed:

- A white candle (for peace and clarity).
- A small bowl of water.
- A sprig of evergreen or rosemary (for renewal).

Steps:

1. Find a quiet space where you won't be disturbed. Dim the lights and light the white candle.

2. Hold the sprig of evergreen or rosemary in your hands and take a few deep breaths, allowing yourself to settle into the moment.

3. Reflect on the stress or burdens you've been carrying. Imagine them flowing into the sprig as you exhale.

4. Dip the sprig into the bowl of water, saying:
"I release what no longer serves me. With this water, I cleanse my spirit and invite peace into my heart."

5. Close your eyes and sit quietly, focusing on the flickering candle flame and visualizing yourself surrounded by a cocoon of light and calm.

2. A Gratitude and Grounding Ritual

Gratitude is a powerful tool for finding peace, grounding your energy, and shifting your perspective during the holiday season.

Materials Needed:

- A journal or blank paper.
- A pen or pencil.
- A small stone or crystal (such as hematite or smoky quartz).

Steps:

1. Begin by holding the stone or crystal in your hands. Take a few deep breaths and feel its grounding energy anchoring you to the Earth.

2. Write down five things you are grateful for this season, focusing on the simple blessings in your life.

3. For each item on your list, pause and reflect on how it makes you feel.

4. Place the journal and the stone on your altar or a sacred space, saying:
"In gratitude, I find my peace. In grounding, I find my strength. So it is."

Repeat this ritual whenever you feel overwhelmed or disconnected.

3. The Yule Light Meditation

This meditation helps you align with the returning light of the Sun and bring a sense of calm and hope into your life.

Materials Needed:

- A gold or yellow candle.
- Soft, instrumental music (optional).

Steps:

1. Sit comfortably in a quiet space and light the candle. Focus on its flame, imagining it as a representation of the Sun's rebirth.
2. Close your eyes and take deep breaths, visualizing the light growing brighter and filling your entire body with warmth and serenity.
3. Repeat an affirmation, such as:
   "With the light of the Sun, I am renewed. Peace flows through me like a river."
4. When ready, blow out the candle, holding onto the feeling of peace it has inspired.

Aligning Your Energy with Yule's Tranquil Vibes

Yule is a season of stillness, introspection, and quiet renewal. Aligning your energy with these qualities helps you flow harmoniously with the natural rhythms of the season, fostering a deeper sense of peace.

1. Connecting with the Energy of the Winter Solstice

The Winter Solstice marks the longest night and shortest day of the year, a time for embracing both darkness and light. To align with this energy:

- Spend time in quiet reflection, journaling about the lessons of the past year.
- Honor the darkness by lighting a single candle, symbolizing the light that guides you through challenging times.
- Meditate on balance, considering how both rest and action contribute to your well-being.

2. Incorporating Restorative Practices

The stillness of Yule invites you to rest and recharge. Incorporate restorative activities into your daily routine:

- Practice gentle yoga or stretching to release physical tension.
- Take a warm bath with calming herbs like chamomile or lavender, visualizing stress melting away.
- Spend time in nature, even if it's a brief walk, to connect with the Earth's quiet energy.

3. Using Seasonal Elements for Peaceful Energy

Enhance your rituals and spaces with items that embody the tranquility of Yule:

- **Crystals:** Use amethyst, blue lace agate, or moonstone for their calming properties.
- **Herbs:** Burn incense or use essential oils like frankincense, cedarwood, or sandalwood to create a peaceful atmosphere.
- **Colors:** Decorate with white, silver, and soft blues to reflect the serene beauty of winter.

4. Creating a Sacred Evening Ritual

End each day with a simple ritual to release stress and cultivate peace:

- Light a candle and place it in a quiet space.
- Write down any worries or frustrations from the day on a small piece of paper.
- Burn the paper in a fireproof dish, saying:
  "As this burns, so too does my stress dissolve. I release it to the universe and welcome peace."
- Sit in stillness for a few moments, focusing on your breath and the flickering candlelight.

The Power of Peace

True peace during the holiday season begins within. By practicing rituals for inner harmony and aligning your energy with the tranquil vibes of Yule, you cultivate a sense of calm that radiates outward, influencing your interactions, your celebrations, and your overall experience of the season.

Yule reminds us that even in the darkest times, light is reborn, and stillness can lead to renewal. Let the rituals and practices in this chapter guide you toward embracing the serene magic of the Winter Solstice, allowing you to move through the season with grace, balance, and a heart full of peace.

Chapter 9: Raising Magical Energy

Yule, the Winter Solstice, is a time of potent spiritual energy and renewal. By coming together in group rituals or gatherings, you can raise and amplify this energy to manifest blessings, promote unity, and foster spiritual growth. When individuals join their intentions, the collective power magnifies, creating a profound and transformative experience.

This chapter explores how to organize and participate in group rituals to raise energy for Yule blessings, offering guidance on harnessing collective power for personal and communal spiritual growth.

Group Rituals and Gatherings to Raise Energy for Yule Blessings

Group rituals are a cornerstone of many spiritual traditions, creating a sense of connection and shared purpose. Yule provides the perfect opportunity to gather with loved ones, coven members, or like-minded individuals to celebrate the season and raise magical energy.

1. Planning a Group Ritual for Yule

A successful group ritual requires intention, organization, and inclusivity. Follow these steps to ensure a harmonious and meaningful experience:

- **Set a Purpose:** Define the goal of the ritual, such as celebrating the return of the Sun, manifesting abundance, or strengthening communal bonds.
- **Choose a Location:** Select a setting that suits the season and your group's preferences, whether it's an indoor sacred space, an outdoor grove, or a cozy living room.
- **Assign Roles:** Designate a facilitator or priest/priestess to guide the ritual. Assign other roles, such as calling the quarters or tending the altar, to ensure everyone is involved.

- **Prepare Materials:** Gather items like candles, incense, drums, ritual tools, and seasonal decorations to enhance the ritual's energy and symbolism.

2. Structure of a Yule Group Ritual
A typical Yule group ritual includes the following elements:

- **Opening the Circle:**
  Begin by casting a sacred circle to create a protected space. Have participants hold hands or walk in a circle while chanting or visualizing a glowing light forming around the group.
  Example chant:
  "Circle of light, circle of love, we cast this space with blessings from above."
- **Calling the Quarters:**
  Invoke the elements to bring balance and energy to the circle. Each participant can face a cardinal direction and recite an invocation:
    - **East (Air):** "Spirits of Air, bring clarity and inspiration."
    - **South (Fire):** "Spirits of Fire, bring passion and renewal."
    - **West (Water):** "Spirits of Water, bring healing and reflection."
    - **North (Earth):** "Spirits of Earth, bring grounding and abundance."
- **Main Ritual Activity:**
  Raise energy collectively by focusing on the ritual's purpose. Ideas include:
    - **Lighting a Communal Yule Log:** Each participant can add a sprig of evergreen to the log and state their intention or blessing.
    - **Drumming and Chanting:** Use rhythmic drumming, clapping, or chanting to build energy. A simple chant like

"The Sun returns, the light will grow, blessings abound, above and below" can be repeated in unison.

- ○ **Energy Raising Circle Dance:** Form a circle and move together, building energy through synchronized movement and shared intent.

- **Sending the Energy:**
Once the energy has reached its peak, direct it toward the group's intention. Visualize the energy as a radiant beam of light flowing toward the goal, whether it's personal growth, community blessings, or healing for the Earth.

- **Closing the Circle:**
Thank the elements and spirits, and release the circle. Encourage participants to share their reflections or feelings from the ritual.

3. Building Energy through Unity and Joy

Group rituals don't have to be solemn—laughter, joy, and connection are powerful ways to raise energy. Incorporate activities like storytelling, singing, or sharing personal blessings to create a positive and uplifting atmosphere.

Harnessing Collective Power for Spiritual Growth

When individuals come together with shared intent, the collective power generated can catalyze profound spiritual transformation. Harnessing this energy requires trust, focus, and mutual respect among participants.

1. The Power of Shared Intention

The strength of a group's energy depends on the clarity and unity of its intentions. To align the group:

- Begin with a discussion or meditation to synchronize your goals and focus.
- Create a shared affirmation or mantra, such as *"Together, we manifest light, love, and renewal."*
- Encourage participants to visualize the same outcome, amplifying the collective intent.

2. Energy-Building Techniques for Groups

- **Chanting and Vocalization:**
  Use repetitive chants, mantras, or toning to harmonize the group's energy. A simple chant like *"We are one, we are whole, we are light within the soul"* can create a sense of unity and focus.
- **Drumming Circles:**
  Drumming is an ancient technique for raising energy. Have participants drum or clap in a steady rhythm, gradually increasing the tempo to build excitement and power.
- **Energy Ball Exercise:**
  Visualize a ball of light forming in the center of the group. Each person contributes their energy to the ball, making it brighter and larger. When the energy peaks, release it together toward the ritual's goal.

3. Balancing Group Energy

Group dynamics can sometimes lead to imbalances, such as one person dominating the energy or others feeling disconnected. To maintain balance:

- Encourage equal participation by giving everyone a role or voice in the ritual.
- Use grounding techniques, like deep breathing or holding hands, to re-center the group if the energy feels chaotic.
- Check in with participants after the ritual to ensure everyone feels supported and valued.

4. Deepening Connections within the Group

A strong sense of community enhances the energy of group rituals. Foster deeper connections through:

- **Shared Meals:** Host a Yule potluck where everyone contributes a dish, symbolizing the group's collective abundance.
- **Gift Exchanges:** Exchange small, meaningful gifts like handmade ornaments or candles to express gratitude for each other.
- **Post-Ritual Reflection:** Create space for participants to share their experiences, insights, or feelings after the ritual.

Practical Considerations for Group Rituals

To ensure a safe and enjoyable experience for all participants:

- Communicate expectations clearly, including the purpose, duration, and any materials needed.
- Be inclusive, respecting diverse beliefs and comfort levels.
- Practice environmental mindfulness by leaving no trace, especially if celebrating outdoors.

The Magic of Raising Energy Together

Group rituals and gatherings at Yule are not only powerful tools for raising energy but also profound opportunities to connect with others on a spiritual level. The collective energy generated by shared intention and effort can manifest blessings far beyond what an individual might achieve alone.

By honoring the season, celebrating together, and harnessing the power of unity, you create a sacred experience that nurtures both personal and communal growth. As the light of the Sun returns, let the bonds formed during these rituals remind you of the strength and magic that arise when we come together in harmony and purpose.

Chapter 10: The Power of Winter Incense and Scents

Scent has a profound effect on our energy, emotions, and spiritual state, making it a powerful tool in any spiritual practice. The aromas of winter, particularly those associated with Yule, evoke warmth, renewal, and connection to the Earth's cycles. By crafting your own Yule incense and oils, you can harness the power of seasonal scents to enhance your rituals, create sacred spaces, and align your energy with the magic of the Winter Solstice.

This chapter delves into the art of creating Yule incense and oils, explores the significance of seasonal aromas, and offers guidance on using them to shift energy and deepen your spiritual connection.

Creating Yule Incense and Oils to Enhance Spiritual Practice

Crafting your own incense and oils allows you to tailor their energy and intent to your specific spiritual goals. The act of blending these aromatic creations is a ritual in itself, infusing them with your intentions for the season.

1. Understanding the Symbolism of Yule Scents

Each ingredient in your incense or oil carries its own energetic properties, enhancing your spiritual practice when used with intention:

- **Frankincense:** Represents purification, protection, and connection to higher realms.
- **Myrrh:** Symbolizes healing, grounding, and spiritual enlightenment.
- **Cinnamon:** Brings warmth, prosperity, and vitality.
- **Pine:** Enhances clarity, renewal, and protection.
- **Clove:** Promotes courage, abundance, and purification.
- **Orange Peel:** Encourages joy, positivity, and solar energy.
- **Juniper Berries:** Offer protection, cleansing, and a connection to the spirit world.

By blending these ingredients, you create a powerful aromatic representation of Yule's themes—light, renewal, and connection.

2. Crafting Yule Incense

Incense can be burned to purify spaces, raise energy, or create a sacred atmosphere for rituals and meditation.

Ingredients for Loose Incense:

- 1 part dried pine needles or resin
- 1 part frankincense resin
- ½ part cinnamon chips or ground cinnamon
- ½ part crushed juniper berries
- ½ part dried orange peel

Instructions:

1. Combine all ingredients in a mortar and pestle. Grind them together while focusing on your intention for the incense (e.g., cleansing, abundance, or connection).
2. Store the mixture in an airtight container.
3. To use, sprinkle a small amount onto a lit charcoal disk placed in a fireproof bowl or burner.

Intentional Use: Burn your Yule incense during rituals, meditation, or gatherings to fill the space with seasonal energy.

3. Crafting Yule Oils

Essential oils capture the essence of seasonal botanicals, making them versatile tools for anointing, diffusing, or adding to candles and baths.

Yule Oil Recipe:

- 4 oz carrier oil (such as jojoba, almond, or olive oil)
- 10 drops frankincense essential oil
- 10 drops orange essential oil
- 5 drops cinnamon essential oil
- 5 drops clove essential oil
- Optional: Add a small piece of pine needle or a juniper berry to the bottle for decoration and energy.

Instructions:

1. Blend the essential oils into the carrier oil, focusing on your intention for the blend.
2. Gently swirl the bottle to mix.
3. Label the bottle with its purpose and store it in a cool, dark place.

Ways to Use Yule Oil:

- Anoint candles, altars, or ritual tools.
- Dab a small amount on your wrists or pulse points during meditation.
- Add a few drops to a diffuser to fill your space with its aroma.

The Power of Seasonal Aromas to Shift Energy

Seasonal scents have a unique ability to evoke memories, emotions, and spiritual states, making them ideal for shifting energy during Yule. By incorporating these aromas into your practice, you can create a sacred environment and align your energy with the season's themes.

1. Cleansing and Purification

Winter scents like pine, juniper, and frankincense are known for their purifying properties. Use these aromas to clear your space of negative energy and create a fresh start:

- **Smoke Cleansing:** Burn pine resin, juniper berries, or frankincense to cleanse your home, altar, or ritual space.
- **Room Spray:** Mix water with a few drops of essential oils like cedarwood and orange in a spray bottle for a quick and effective cleansing mist.

2. Raising Energy

Cinnamon, clove, and orange are warming, uplifting scents that invigorate the spirit and raise energy levels. Incorporate these aromas to amplify your rituals:

- Add a cinnamon stick and orange peel to a simmer pot of water on your stove.
- Use a diffuser with an energizing blend of orange, cinnamon, and clove oils.
- Anoint candles with Yule oil before lighting them to intensify their energy.

3. Fostering Inner Peace and Reflection

Scents like myrrh, sandalwood, and lavender promote calm and introspection, aligning you with Yule's tranquil energy. Use these aromas to foster a sense of inner peace:

- Burn myrrh or sandalwood incense during meditation or journaling.
- Add lavender and frankincense oils to a warm bath for a relaxing ritual.
- Diffuse calming blends in your space to encourage restful sleep and quiet reflection.

4. Creating Sacred Space

Scent is a key element in establishing a sacred atmosphere for rituals, celebrations, or personal practice.

- Before a ritual, use Yule incense to cleanse and consecrate the space.
- Light candles scented with pine, cinnamon, or orange to set the mood for your celebrations.
- Place aromatic bundles of herbs like rosemary and pine on your altar to infuse it with seasonal energy.

5. Enhancing Manifestation

Certain scents are particularly effective for manifestation, helping you align your intentions with the energy of Yule:

- Use frankincense and orange oils to focus on abundance and success.
- Incorporate clove and cinnamon into spells for courage and empowerment.
- Combine juniper and myrrh for rituals centered on spiritual growth and renewal.

Seasonal Scents for Everyday Use

You don't need to limit the use of Yule scents to formal rituals. Incorporate them into your daily life to maintain a connection to the season's energy:

- Add a few drops of Yule oil to your morning skincare routine for a grounding start to the day.
- Place sachets filled with dried herbs like cinnamon, clove, and pine in drawers or closets for a constant reminder of the season.
- Use seasonal candles or potpourri to fill your home with the aromas of Yule.

The Magic of Aromas

The scents of Yule hold transformative power, connecting us to the magic of the season and enhancing every aspect of our spiritual practice. Whether crafting your own incense and oils or using pre-made blends, these aromas can cleanse, energize, and uplift, aligning your spirit with the warmth and renewal of the Winter Solstice.

By intentionally working with seasonal scents, you create an environment that nurtures your body, mind, and soul, allowing the magic of Yule to permeate every corner of your life. Let these aromas be your guide as you journey through the season, bringing peace, joy, and light to your sacred spaces and beyond.

Chapter 11: Yule Log Traditions

The Yule log is one of the most enduring symbols of the Winter Solstice, steeped in history, ritual, and magical significance. Originally a Norse and Celtic tradition, the Yule log was burned to honor the returning Sun, protect the home, and invoke prosperity for the coming year. Today, the Yule log remains a beloved feature of Yule celebrations, representing light, warmth, and the cycle of renewal.

In this chapter, we'll explore the history and ritual significance of the Yule log, provide detailed instructions for crafting your own, and offer guidance on performing rituals involving the burning of the Yule log to attract prosperity, protection, and blessings.

Crafting Your Own Yule Log: History and Ritual Significance

The Yule log originated in pre-Christian Europe, where it was central to midwinter celebrations. Burning a large log in the hearth symbolized the triumph of light over darkness and was believed to protect the household from misfortune. Over time, this tradition evolved, incorporating magical and spiritual elements that endure in modern practices.

1. The Historical Significance of the Yule Log

The Yule log was more than a festive decoration—it was a sacred object imbued with intention and reverence. Key aspects of its history include:

- **Norse Traditions:** In Norse mythology, the Yule log honored Thor, the god of thunder, and celebrated the Sun's rebirth after the longest night.
- **Celtic Practices:** For the Celts, the burning of oak logs symbolized strength and protection, as oak was considered a sacred tree with divine energy.
- **European Customs:** In medieval Europe, families would gather to burn a large log on the hearth, sprinkling it with wine, salt, or oil as offerings to ensure a bountiful year ahead.

The ashes of the Yule log were often collected and scattered in fields to promote fertility or kept in the home as a protective charm.

2. Crafting a Modern Yule Log

Making your own Yule log is a meaningful way to connect with this ancient tradition and personalize it for your spiritual practice.

Materials Needed:

- A log from a tree that holds significance to you (oak, pine, or birch are traditional).
- Evergreen branches (e.g., holly, pine, or ivy).
- Seasonal decorations like dried orange slices, cinnamon sticks, or ribbons in Yule colors (red, green, gold, or white).
- Candles (optional): Red, green, or gold taper candles or tealights for decoration and ritual use.

Steps:

1. **Select the Log:** Choose a log that fits your space and purpose. If burning indoors, ensure it is appropriately sized for your fireplace. If not burning, a decorative log can serve as a centerpiece or altar item.
2. **Decorate the Log:** Wrap evergreen branches around the log and secure them with twine or ribbon. Add dried fruits, cinnamon sticks, or other natural embellishments.
3. **Add Candle Holders:** For a decorative Yule log, carve or attach spaces for candles. Arrange the candles to represent the Sun's rebirth and the returning light.
4. **Infuse with Intention:** Hold the log and focus on the blessings you wish to manifest, such as prosperity, protection, or harmony. You can also anoint the log with oils like frankincense or cedar for added energy.

Magical Tip: If possible, harvest the log and decorations respectfully from nature, asking permission and giving thanks to the trees and land.

Burning the Yule Log for Prosperity and Protection

The burning of the Yule log is a symbolic act that connects you with the cycles of light and darkness, invoking the blessings of renewal and abundance. Whether performed alone or with loved ones, this ritual brings warmth, hope, and magic to your Yule celebration.

1. Preparing for the Yule Log Ritual

Before burning your Yule log, prepare a sacred space and gather your intentions.

Materials Needed:

- Your crafted Yule log.
- Matches or a lighter.
- Incense or smudge sticks for cleansing.
- A small bowl of salt or water for protection.
- A written list of intentions or blessings for the coming year.

Steps:

1. Cleanse the space and the Yule log with incense or smoke, setting the stage for the ritual.
2. Place the Yule log in the hearth or firepit, ensuring it is safe and secure for burning.
3. If desired, sprinkle the log with wine, oil, or herbs as an offering to the Sun or your chosen deities.

2. The Burning Ritual
Lighting the Log:

1. Gather around the hearth with family or friends, or perform the ritual alone in quiet reflection.
2. Light the Yule log, saying:
   "As this log burns, so too does the darkness fade. With its warmth, we welcome the Sun's return, and with its light, we manifest joy, prosperity, and protection."

Raising Energy:

- As the fire grows, visualize its flames carrying your intentions into the universe.
- Chant or sing as a group to raise energy. A simple chant might be: *"Light returns, the Sun will rise, blessings flow from Earth and skies."*

3. Using the Yule Log Ashes
The ashes of the Yule log are believed to hold protective and magical properties. After the fire has burned out:

- Scatter the ashes in your garden or around your home to promote fertility and protection.
- Keep a small amount in a pouch or jar on your altar as a charm for prosperity and good luck throughout the year.

4. Alternative Yule Log Practices

If you don't have access to a fireplace or outdoor firepit, you can adapt the Yule log tradition:

- **Decorative Yule Log:** Create a non-burning centerpiece for your table or altar, using candles to symbolize the flames.
- **Virtual Ritual:** Share the Yule log tradition with friends or family through a virtual gathering, lighting candles simultaneously to honor the Sun's return.

Symbolism and Spiritual Meaning

The Yule log is more than a physical object; it is a representation of the cyclical nature of life, the balance of darkness and light, and the hope for renewal. Each part of the tradition carries profound meaning:

- **The Log:** Represents the tree of life, strength, and endurance.
- **The Flames:** Symbolize the rebirth of the Sun and the triumph of light.
- **The Ashes:** Embody transformation, renewal, and the fertility of the Earth.

Integrating Yule Log Traditions into Modern Life

Even in today's world, the Yule log tradition offers an opportunity to pause, reflect, and reconnect with ancient wisdom. By crafting and burning a Yule log, you create a moment of sacred ritual that honors the past, celebrates the present, and sets intentions for the future.

As you watch the flames dance and feel the warmth of the fire, remember that this ancient custom carries the energy of countless generations who have celebrated the return of the light. Let it inspire you to find strength, joy, and renewal in the season of Yule.

Chapter 12: True Love Spells and Charms

Yule, the Winter Solstice, is a time of renewal, connection, and warmth. As the longest night gives way to the returning light of the Sun, it also opens a portal for strengthening love and deepening relationships. The magical energy of Yule is ideal for casting spells to foster love, connection, and harmony in your relationships—whether romantic, familial, or platonic. By channeling this energy into handmade charms, you create tangible symbols of love and devotion.

This chapter delves into casting spells for love and connection during Yule and provides detailed guidance on crafting handmade charms to nurture and strengthen relationships.

Casting Spells for Love and Connection during Yule

Love spells during Yule focus on fostering genuine connections, strengthening existing bonds, and attracting love into your life. These spells align with the season's themes of warmth, renewal, and light.

1. Preparing for a Yule Love Spell

Before casting any spell, it's essential to prepare your space and intentions:

- **Cleanse Your Space:** Use incense, smudging herbs, or sound to clear away negative energy.
- **Gather Supplies:** Collect candles, crystals, herbs, and other tools that resonate with love and connection.
- **Set Your Intention:** Focus on your desired outcome, whether it's attracting love, healing a relationship, or deepening a bond. Be specific and authentic in your intentions.
- **Align with the Energy of Yule:** Reflect on the themes of light and renewal, channeling these energies into your spell.

2. Yule Candle Love Spell

This simple but powerful spell uses candle magic to attract love or strengthen an existing relationship.

Materials Needed:

- A red or pink candle (for love and passion)
- A white candle (for purity and harmony)
- Rose petals or lavender (for love and peace)
- A small piece of paper and a pen
- Optional: Rose quartz crystal

Steps:

1. **Prepare the Candles:** Carve your name and your intention (e.g., love, connection, harmony) into the red or pink candle. Anoint the candle with rose oil or another love-related oil if desired.
2. **Set the Space:** Arrange the white and red/pink candles on your altar or table. Sprinkle rose petals or lavender around them.
3. **Focus Your Intention:** On the piece of paper, write your intention or a specific wish for love or connection. Fold the paper and place it beneath the red/pink candle.
4. **Light the Candles:** First light the white candle, saying:
   "With purity and light, I call forth love and harmony."
   Then light the red or pink candle, saying:
   "With passion and warmth, I welcome love and connection into my life."
5. **Meditate:** Spend time gazing at the flames, visualizing your intention manifesting. Feel the warmth of the candles filling your heart with love and joy.
6. **Close the Spell:** Allow the candles to burn out safely, or extinguish them with gratitude. Keep the folded paper as a talisman or bury it in the Earth to seal your intention.

3. The Yule Love Knot Spell

This spell strengthens bonds between you and a loved one by weaving intentions of love, trust, and connection into a simple knot.

Materials Needed:

- A red or pink ribbon (for love and passion)
- A white ribbon (for harmony and clarity)
- Optional: A charm or token representing the relationship

Steps:

1. Hold the ribbons in your hands and take a few deep breaths, focusing on your intention.
2. Begin tying knots in the ribbons, saying a blessing or affirmation with each knot:
   - **First Knot:** *"With this knot, I weave trust and connection."*
   - **Second Knot:** *"With this knot, I strengthen love and harmony."*
   - **Third Knot:** *"With this knot, I bind us with light and joy."*
3. Attach the charm or token to the knotted ribbons if desired.
4. Place the ribbons on your altar, carry them as a talisman, or give them to the person you're focusing on.

Handmade Charms to Strengthen Relationships

Charms are tangible representations of your love and intentions, making them powerful tools for strengthening relationships. Handmade charms infuse your personal energy into the object, enhancing their effectiveness and meaning.

1. Heart Sachets for Love and Harmony

Create a sachet filled with herbs and symbols of love to attract or strengthen relationships.

Materials Needed:

- A small red or pink cloth pouch (or fabric to sew your own)
- Dried herbs such as rose petals, lavender, and chamomile
- A small rose quartz or amethyst crystal
- A ribbon to close the pouch

Steps:

1. Place the herbs and crystal in the pouch, focusing on your intention as you do so.
2. Hold the filled pouch in your hands and say:
   "This charm carries love, harmony, and connection. May it strengthen the bonds between us."
3. Close the pouch with the ribbon and keep it near your bed, on your altar, or give it to your loved one.

2. Love Connection Bracelets

Craft simple bracelets to symbolize the connection between you and a loved one.

Materials Needed:

- String or cord in red, pink, or white
- Small beads or charms that symbolize your relationship (e.g., hearts, initials, or birthstones)

Steps:

1. Thread the beads onto the cord, focusing on the love and connection you wish to strengthen.
2. Tie the bracelet with a secure knot, saying:
   "As I tie this knot, our bond grows stronger. Love flows between us like an endless river."
3. Wear the bracelet yourself or gift it to your loved one.

3. Yule Ornament Charm

Turn a Yule ornament into a charm that strengthens your family or romantic bond.

Materials Needed:

- A clear glass or plastic ornament (fillable)
- Small items like rose petals, glitter, cinnamon sticks, and hand-written affirmations of love
- Ribbon or string for hanging

Steps:

1. Fill the ornament with the items, layering them with care and intention.
2. Seal the ornament and tie it with a ribbon, saying:
   "This charm carries the light of Yule, bringing love and connection to all who gather here."
3. Hang the ornament on your Yule tree or in a prominent place in your home.

Integrating Love Spells and Charms into Your Yule Celebration

The power of Yule is amplified when you incorporate love spells and charms into your seasonal traditions. Here are some ways to integrate them into your celebration:

- Perform a love spell as part of a group ritual or family gathering, focusing on strengthening your collective bond.
- Create handmade charms together as an act of love and connection.

• Share your charms as heartfelt gifts, spreading the energy of love and harmony to those around you.

The Magic of Love during Yule

The true magic of love spells and charms lies not in manipulation but in intention—fostering connections, nurturing trust, and creating space for joy and harmony to flourish. Yule, with its themes of warmth and renewal, provides the perfect backdrop for these practices.

As you craft charms or cast spells, remember that the energy you put forth will ripple outward, enhancing the love in your relationships and the world around you. Through these acts of intention and creativity, you honor the light and love that are at the heart of Yule and all your connections.

Chapter 13: The Magic of Music and Song

Music and sound have been integral to spiritual practices for millennia, offering a powerful way to raise energy, create sacred space, and connect with the divine. During Yule, the Winter Solstice, the magic of music resonates deeply, reflecting the season's themes of renewal, celebration, and connection. Whether through songs, chants, drumming, or instrumental melodies, music enhances your rituals, gatherings, and personal reflections, aligning your energy with the transformative magic of Yule.

This chapter explores how to create sacred sounds for Yule through songs, chants, and drumming and provides techniques for using vibrational magic to enhance your Yule rituals.

Creating Sacred Sounds for Yule: Songs, Chants, and Drumming

Sacred sounds amplify the energy of your Yule celebrations, bringing joy, focus, and harmony to your spiritual practices. By incorporating music, chants, and rhythms into your rituals, you create a shared experience that resonates with the season's themes of light and renewal.

1. The Power of Sacred Songs

Singing is one of the most ancient and accessible forms of spiritual expression. Songs for Yule can honor the Sun's return, celebrate the changing seasons, or express gratitude for life's blessings.

Traditional Yule Song Themes:

- **The Sun's Rebirth:** Celebrate the return of light after the longest night of the year.
- **Connection with Nature:** Sing about the beauty of winter landscapes, evergreen trees, and the cycles of life.
- **Community and Gratitude:** Use music to strengthen bonds with loved ones and give thanks for their presence.

Example Yule Song:
"The Light Returns"
(Tune of your choice or simple chant style)
"The light returns, the Sun will rise,
Warmth and hope fill winter skies.
We welcome back the golden flame,
In every heart, it shines the same."

Sing this song during a Yule gathering or while lighting candles on your altar to invoke the energy of renewal and hope.

2. Crafting Yule Chants

Chants are simple, repetitive phrases set to rhythm or melody, making them ideal for group rituals or personal meditation. The repetition focuses the mind and raises energy, creating a powerful spiritual experience.

Creating Your Own Chant:

- Choose a theme, such as renewal, protection, or gratitude.
- Use short, rhythmic phrases that are easy to remember.
- Incorporate seasonal imagery, such as fire, evergreen trees, or the turning wheel of the year.

Example Chant:
"Fire burn, the wheel will turn,
The Sun returns, the light will burn."

Repeat this chant during a ritual while circling a fire or holding hands with loved ones to raise energy and set intentions.

3. Drumming and Percussion

Drumming is an ancient tool for raising energy and connecting with the rhythm of the Earth. The steady beat of a drum mirrors the heartbeat, grounding participants and aligning their energy with the natural cycles.

Using Drumming in Yule Rituals:

- **Opening a Ritual:** Begin with slow, steady drumming to ground the group and set the tone for the ritual.
- **Raising Energy:** Gradually increase the tempo and intensity to build excitement and amplify collective energy.
- **Closing the Ritual:** Return to a slow, calming beat to bring the group back to a state of peace and reflection.

If you don't have a drum, use alternative percussion instruments like rattles, tambourines, or even clapping and stomping to create rhythmic sound.

4. Incorporating Instrumental Music

Instrumental music can evoke the season's mood and support the energy of your rituals. Choose music that resonates with the themes of Yule:

- **String Instruments:** Harps, violins, and acoustic guitars produce soft, melodic sounds that encourage introspection and peace.
- **Wind Instruments:** Flutes and panpipes evoke the winter wind and connect you to the natural world.
- **Bells and Chimes:** Create a crisp, clear tone that symbolizes the purity of snow and the ringing in of a new season.

Play instrumental music softly in the background of your rituals, meditations, or gatherings to create a serene and sacred atmosphere.

Enhancing Yule Rituals with Vibrational Magic

The vibrations of sound have a profound effect on energy, emotions, and the spiritual environment. By using sound intentionally, you can deepen your connection to the season's magic and amplify the power of your rituals.

1. Sound Cleansing for Yule

Sound is a powerful tool for clearing stagnant or negative energy, making it ideal for preparing your space for Yule celebrations.

Techniques for Sound Cleansing:

- **Bell Ringing:** Walk through your space ringing a small bell, focusing on dispersing negativity and inviting in light.
- **Singing Bowl:** Use a singing bowl to create soothing, resonant tones that purify the energy of your ritual area.
- **Clapping:** Simple clapping in corners or near doorways breaks up dense energy and clears the air.

Combine sound cleansing with incense or smudging for a comprehensive energy reset.

2. Aligning with the Energy of the Solstice

The Winter Solstice is a time for stillness, introspection, and renewal. Use sound to align with these energies during meditation or personal rituals.

Sound Meditation:

1. Sit in a quiet space and light a candle to represent the returning light.
2. Play soft, instrumental music or create your own tones using a singing bowl or humming.

3. Focus on the vibrations, imagining them aligning your energy with the cycles of nature and the cosmos.

3. Raising Group Energy with Sound

For group rituals, sound can unify participants and create a shared energy field.

Group Drumming Circle:

- Have each participant bring a drum or percussion instrument.
- Begin with a slow, steady beat, gradually increasing tempo as energy builds.
- Encourage participants to improvise rhythms or harmonize with the group.

Call-and-Response Chants:

- One person leads with a phrase, and the group repeats it.
- Example:
    - Leader: "The light returns!"
    - Group: "The Sun will rise!"

This interaction fosters connection and amplifies the group's intention.

4. Using Sound to Seal Intentions

Once a ritual or meditation is complete, sound can be used to seal your intentions and release the energy into the universe.

- Ring a bell or chime three times.
- End with a group chant or song to express gratitude.
- Strike a drum or singing bowl to mark the conclusion of the ritual.

Integrating Music into Everyday Yule Practices

You don't need a formal ritual to enjoy the magic of music during Yule. Incorporate sacred sounds into your daily life to maintain a connection to the season's energy:

- **Morning Devotions:** Begin your day with a chant or song to set a positive tone.
- **Family Gatherings:** Sing traditional Yule songs or play instrumental music to enhance the festive atmosphere.
- **Personal Reflection:** Use drumming or instrumental music to accompany your journaling or meditation.

The Magic of Music during Yule

Music and sound are powerful allies in your spiritual practice, offering a way to connect with the essence of Yule on a vibrational level. Whether through songs, chants, drumming, or instrumental melodies, the magic of music enhances your rituals, deepens your connections, and aligns your energy with the cycles of the season.

As you sing, drum, or hum, remember that sound transcends time and space, carrying your intentions into the universe. Let the music of Yule fill your heart with joy, hope, and renewal, echoing the timeless harmony of the Winter Solstice.

Chapter 14: The Joy of Handmade Wrapping

Gift-giving during Yule is a celebration of love, gratitude, and connection, but the wrapping of a gift carries its own magic. Handmade wrapping transforms the act of giving into a sacred ritual, infusing your offerings with intention, care, and creativity. Beyond aesthetics, eco-friendly and magically charged wrapping connects you with nature's cycles, aligns your gifts with Yule's themes, and makes each present truly meaningful.

In this chapter, we explore eco-friendly and magically charged wrapping ideas and offer guidance on personalizing gift wrapping to create a lasting impression and a deeper connection during Yule.

Eco-Friendly and Magically Charged Wrapping Ideas

Handmade and sustainable wrapping not only protects the environment but also imbues your gifts with positive energy and intention. By choosing natural materials and incorporating magical elements, you create wrapping that aligns with Yule's themes of renewal and abundance.

1. Sustainable Wrapping Materials

Use materials that are eco-friendly and reusable, avoiding waste and honoring the Earth's cycles.

Ideas for Eco-Friendly Wrapping:

- **Fabric Wrapping (Furoshiki):** Use squares of fabric, scarves, or cloth napkins to wrap gifts. This Japanese-inspired method is reusable and elegant.
- **Brown Kraft Paper:** Simple and biodegradable, kraft paper serves as a blank canvas for creative decoration.
- **Recycled Paper:** Repurpose old maps, sheet music, newspaper, or pages from damaged books for unique and sustainable wrapping.
- **Reusable Bags:** Sew small fabric pouches or use cloth tote bags that can be reused by the recipient.

- **Natural Elements:** Incorporate twine, raffia, or jute instead of synthetic ribbons, and decorate with sprigs of evergreen, pinecones, or cinnamon sticks.

2. Magically Charged Wrapping Techniques

Infuse your wrapping process with intention and magical energy to create spiritually meaningful gifts.

Blessing the Wrapping Materials:

- Before wrapping, cleanse your materials with incense or a smudge stick, saying:
  "May this wrapping carry light and love, bringing joy and blessings to its recipient."
- Visualize the materials glowing with positive energy as you work.

Choosing Colors with Intention:

- Red: Passion, love, vitality.
- Green: Growth, renewal, prosperity.
- Gold: Abundance, light, success.
- White: Purity, peace, clarity.

Incorporating Symbols:

- Paint or draw Yule-themed symbols (stars, holly, spirals) on paper.
- Use stamps or stencils to add designs like the Sun, snowflakes, or trees.
- Write blessings or affirmations on the inside of the wrapping paper before covering the gift.

3. Nature-Inspired Decorations

Bring the energy of Yule into your wrapping by incorporating natural elements:

- **Evergreens:** Tuck sprigs of pine, cedar, or holly under twine or ribbons for protection and renewal.
- **Herbs:** Add dried rosemary or lavender for calming and healing energy.
- **Cinnamon Sticks:** Symbolize warmth and prosperity; tie them to packages with twine.
- **Pinecones and Acorns:** Represent abundance and grounding; use them as decorative accents.

These additions not only enhance the appearance of your gifts but also connect them to the Earth's energy.

Personalizing Gift Wrapping for a Meaningful Yule

Personalized wrapping adds a heartfelt touch to your gifts, showing the recipient that you've put thought and care into every detail. Each package becomes a unique expression of your connection to the person and the spirit of Yule.

1. Adding a Personal Touch

Tailor your wrapping to reflect the recipient's personality, interests, or shared memories:

- **Custom Tags:** Create gift tags using cardstock or recycled paper. Decorate with the recipient's name, zodiac sign, or a meaningful symbol.
- **Photo Wrapping:** Print small photos of shared memories and attach them to the gift.
- **Handwritten Notes:** Write a personal blessing, wish, or affirmation on the wrapping paper or a small card tucked into the ribbon.

2. Incorporating Magical Intentions

Transform your wrapping into a charm or talisman by embedding magical elements:

- **Sigils:** Draw a sigil for love, abundance, or protection on the underside of the wrapping paper or on the ribbon.
- **Crystals:** Attach a small crystal, such as rose quartz for love or citrine for prosperity, to the gift as an added blessing.
- **Herbal Infusions:** Sprinkle a small amount of dried herbs (like chamomile for peace or basil for abundance) inside the wrapping paper.

3. Themed Wrapping Ideas

Create thematic wrapping designs that align with Yule's energy:

- **The Sun's Return:** Use gold paper, draw or stamp Sun symbols, and tie with yellow ribbon to honor the rebirth of light.
- **Evergreen Forest:** Wrap with green fabric or paper, decorate with tiny pinecones and sprigs of fir, and include a woodland-inspired charm.
- **Snow and Stars:** Use white or silver wrapping, add star or snowflake decorations, and sprinkle with eco-friendly glitter for a wintry effect.

4. Wrapping as a Ritual

Approach the act of wrapping as a sacred ritual, focusing on your intentions and the energy you wish to share:

- **Create a Sacred Space:** Light a candle and play calming music as you gather your materials.
- **Focus Your Intentions:** Hold the gift and visualize the recipient's joy and blessings as you wrap it.
- **Seal the Energy:** Tie the package with a bow or ribbon, saying: *"This gift is wrapped with love and light, bringing blessings to [recipient's name] on this sacred night."*

5. Wrapping for Community and Connection

If you're wrapping gifts for a group, such as family or a coven, consider creating a unifying theme that reflects your shared connection:

- Use matching colors or materials for all gifts to symbolize unity.
- Add a small charm or token to each package that represents your shared bond (e.g., a tiny star for hope, a bell for joy).
- Incorporate shared symbols or intentions that honor the group's collective energy.

Eco-Friendly Disposal and Reuse

Encourage recipients to reuse or recycle the wrapping materials to extend their life and reduce waste:

- Suggest reusing fabric or ribbons for future gifts.
- Offer ideas for repurposing natural decorations, such as adding herbs or evergreens to compost.
- If using paper, ensure it's recyclable or biodegradable.

The Magic of Handmade Wrapping

The act of wrapping a gift is often overlooked, but it carries immense potential for creativity, magic, and connection. By choosing eco-friendly materials, adding personal touches, and infusing your wrapping with intention, you transform a simple act into a meaningful expression of love and gratitude.

As you prepare your Yule gifts, let the joy of handmade wrapping remind you of the deeper purpose of the season—sharing light, fostering connection, and celebrating the beauty of the natural world. Each carefully wrapped gift becomes a reflection of your heart and a tribute to the magic of Yule.

Chapter 15: Candle Magic for Yule

Candle magic, one of the simplest yet most potent forms of spell-work, is a perfect practice for Yule, the Winter Solstice. As the longest night of the year gives way to the returning light of the Sun, candles symbolize hope, renewal, and transformation. The act of lighting a candle is both a physical and spiritual gesture, embodying the themes of Yule: warmth, illumination, and the triumph of light over darkness.

This chapter explores candle rituals that align with Yule's energy and offers guidance on using candle magic to manifest your intentions for the season.

Lighting the Path to the Sun: Candle Rituals for Renewal and Hope

Yule marks the rebirth of the Sun, making candle rituals especially meaningful. By lighting candles with intention, you honor the return of light and create space for renewal in your life.

1. Preparing for Candle Rituals

Before performing any candle ritual, prepare your space, tools, and energy:

- **Cleanse Your Space:** Use incense, sage, or sound to purify the area where you'll perform the ritual.
- **Choose Your Candles:** Select candles in colors that resonate with your intentions. For Yule, popular choices include:
    - **Gold or Yellow:** Represents the returning Sun, abundance, and joy.
    - **Red:** Symbolizes love, vitality, and passion.
    - **Green:** Reflects growth, renewal, and prosperity.
    - **White:** Signifies purity, peace, and clarity.
- **Gather Supplies:** You may also need oils for anointing, herbs, crystals, or holders for safety.

2. The Yule Sun Candle Ritual

This ritual honors the rebirth of the Sun and invites its light into your life and home.

Materials Needed:

- A large gold or yellow candle
- A sprig of evergreen (pine, cedar, or holly)
- A bowl of water or salt for grounding
- Optional: Sun-themed charms or decorations

Steps:

1. Place the candle in the center of your altar or a safe location. Arrange the evergreen sprig and bowl of water or salt around it.
2. Light the candle, saying:
   "On this longest night, I honor the return of the Sun. As its light grows, so too does hope, warmth, and renewal in my life."
3. Spend a few moments gazing into the flame, reflecting on the light's power to dispel darkness. Visualize the flame igniting your own inner light and potential.
4. Leave the candle to burn safely for a while, or extinguish it and re-light it daily throughout the Yule season.

3. Candle Meditation for Hope and Renewal

This meditation focuses on finding inner peace and setting intentions for growth in the coming year.

Materials Needed:

- A white or green candle
- Quiet space for reflection

Steps:

1. Light the candle and sit comfortably in front of it.
2. Focus on the flame, letting its gentle movement draw you into a state of calm.
3. Reflect on areas of your life that feel stagnant or in need of renewal. As you breathe deeply, imagine the flame burning away obstacles and creating space for new growth.
4. Say a simple affirmation, such as:
   "With this light, I release the past and welcome renewal. Hope and joy grow within me."
5. Close the meditation by thanking the flame and extinguishing the candle.

Using Candle Magic to Manifest Your Yule Intentions

Candle magic involves focusing your energy and intention on the flame, turning a simple act of lighting a candle into a powerful spell. The flame acts as a bridge between the physical and spiritual realms, carrying your desires into the universe.

1. Crafting Your Candle Spell

To create a candle spell, follow these steps:

Choose the Right Candle:

- Select a candle color and size that corresponds to your intention. For example:
    - **Gold or Yellow:** For success, joy, and creativity.
    - **Red:** For love, courage, and vitality.
    - **Green:** For growth, wealth, and fertility.
    - **Blue:** For healing, peace, and clarity.

Anoint the Candle:

- Use oils that resonate with your intention, such as:
    - Cinnamon or clove for prosperity.
    - Lavender or rose for love and harmony.
    - Frankincense or cedar for spiritual connection.
- Rub the oil onto the candle from the center outward, focusing on your goal as you work.

Carve Symbols:

- Carve words, symbols, or sigils into the wax that represent your intention. For example:
    - A Sun or spiral for renewal.
    - A heart for love.
    - A dollar sign for abundance.

Add Corresponding Elements:

- Surround the candle with herbs, crystals, or charms that align with your goal.

2. Performing a Yule Candle Spell

Once your candle is prepared, perform the spell with focus and intention.

Steps:

1. **Create Sacred Space:** Cleanse and prepare your space, ensuring you won't be disturbed.
2. **Light the Candle:** Hold your intention in your mind as you light the candle. Visualize your desire as though it has already come to fruition.
3. **Focus on the Flame:** Spend time gazing at the flame, allowing it to draw your energy and intention outward. Say a specific affirmation or incantation, such as:

   "As this flame burns bright and strong, my will is heard, my path is long. Light returns, my goals align, this spell is cast, its power divine."
4. **Let the Candle Burn Safely:** Allow the candle to burn completely if possible, or extinguish it with gratitude and relight it over several days.

3. Candle Magic for Specific Yule Intentions

Here are examples of candle spells tailored to common Yule themes:

For Prosperity:

- Use a green candle anointed with cinnamon oil.
- Surround it with coins, bay leaves, and a citrine crystal.
- Say:
  "With this flame, abundance grows. Wealth and blessings freely flow."

For Love and Connection:

- Use a red or pink candle anointed with rose oil.
- Carve hearts or the initials of loved ones into the wax.
- Say:
  "Love surrounds me, pure and bright. Hearts are warmed on this Yule night."

For Protection:

- Use a black or white candle anointed with frankincense oil.
- Add salt or protective herbs like rosemary or sage around the base.
- Say:
  "With this light, I cast a shield. Harm is banished, blessings revealed."

4. Safeguarding Candle Magic

Safety is essential when working with candles:

- Never leave a burning candle unattended.
- Place candles on a fireproof surface away from flammable objects.
- Use appropriate holders to catch wax drips.

Integrating Candle Magic into Your Yule Celebrations

Candle magic can be woven into every aspect of your Yule celebrations:

- **Group Rituals:** Have each participant light a candle and state an intention, creating a collective web of energy.
- **Decorations:** Place candle arrangements on your Yule altar or dinner table to set a sacred and festive mood.
- **Daily Practice:** Light a single candle each evening during Yule to honor the returning light and reflect on your goals.

The Transformative Power of Candle Magic

Candle magic is a simple yet profound way to honor the energy of Yule. Each flickering flame represents hope, warmth, and the promise of renewal, mirroring the Sun's journey as it begins to grow stronger after the Solstice.

As you light your candles this Yule, let their flames guide your intentions, illuminate your path, and remind you of the infinite power of light to dispel darkness. Whether you seek love, abundance, or peace, the magic of candles will carry your desires into the universe, helping you manifest a brighter and more fulfilling future.

Chapter 16: Yule Blessings and Gratitude

Yule, the Winter Solstice, is a season of reflection and renewal, making it the perfect time to honor the blessings of the past year and express gratitude. The act of offering thanks strengthens your connection to the cycles of nature, the divine, and the people who enrich your life. Moreover, sharing Yule blessings with your community fosters unity, love, and support, amplifying the spirit of the season.

This chapter explores rituals to express gratitude for the year's blessings and provides meaningful ways to share Yule blessings with your community.

Rituals to Offer Thanks for the Year's Blessings

Gratitude is a powerful spiritual practice that deepens your connection with abundance and peace. Yule rituals for gratitude focus on reflecting on the past year, celebrating achievements, and honoring the gifts—both big and small—that have enriched your life.

1. Preparing for Gratitude Rituals

Before performing a gratitude ritual, take time to reflect on the past year:

- **Journal:** Write down events, experiences, and people that brought joy, growth, or lessons into your life.
- **Create a Gratitude List:** Highlight specific blessings, from major milestones to everyday moments of beauty or kindness.
- **Set Your Intention:** Focus on expressing genuine gratitude and honoring the energy that has supported you throughout the year.

2. The Yule Gratitude Candle Ritual

This ritual combines candle magic with heartfelt gratitude, creating a moment to reflect on the year's blessings and set intentions for the future.

Materials Needed:

- A white or gold candle (symbolizing gratitude and light)
- A piece of paper and pen
- A small bowl of water or earth for grounding

Steps:

1. **Prepare Your Space:** Cleanse your space with incense or sound, creating a peaceful atmosphere.
2. **Reflect and Write:** Sit quietly and reflect on the past year. Write down three things you are most grateful for.
3. **Light the Candle:** Place the candle in a safe holder and light it, saying:
   "With this flame, I honor the blessings of the past year. I give thanks for the light that guides me and the abundance that fills my life."
4. **Offer Gratitude:** Hold the paper with your gratitude list and read it aloud. Visualize the light of the candle amplifying your thanks and sending it into the universe.
5. **Ground and Close:** Dip your fingers in the bowl of water or touch the earth, grounding your energy. Extinguish the candle with gratitude.

3. The Blessing Bowl Ritual

This ritual uses a bowl to symbolize the overflowing abundance of your life.

Materials Needed:

- A bowl (preferably made of natural materials like wood or clay)
- Small tokens representing your blessings (stones, coins, herbs, etc.)
- A white cloth or scarf

Steps:

1. **Prepare the Bowl:** Place the bowl in the center of your altar or sacred space. Surround it with candles or decorations that symbolize abundance.
2. **Add Tokens:** For each blessing you wish to honor, place a token in the bowl, saying:
   "I give thanks for [blessing]. May this gratitude return to the Earth and universe, multiplying the light."
3. **Cover the Bowl:** Once filled, cover the bowl with the white cloth as a symbol of preservation and protection for your blessings.
4. **Keep on Your Altar:** Leave the bowl on your altar throughout Yule as a reminder of the abundance in your life.

4. The Gratitude Tree Ritual

This interactive ritual is perfect for families or groups, encouraging collective gratitude.

Materials Needed:

- A small tree or branches arranged in a vase
- Paper cutouts in seasonal shapes (stars, leaves, snowflakes)
- Pens, markers, or crayons

Steps:

1. **Create the Tree:** Set up the tree or branches in your home as a centerpiece.
2. **Write Blessings:** Have each participant write one or more things they are grateful for on the paper cutouts. Decorate them if desired.
3. **Hang on the Tree:** Attach the cutouts to the branches, creating a gratitude tree.
4. **Share as a Group:** Gather around the tree to read aloud your blessings, celebrating the collective abundance.

How to Share Yule Blessings with Your Community

The spirit of Yule extends beyond personal reflection; it is a time to share your light with others. Acts of kindness and generosity not only uplift those around you but also create a ripple effect of positivity.

1. Hosting a Yule Blessing Circle

A blessing circle is a communal ritual where participants gather to share blessings and intentions.

Steps to Host a Circle:

1. **Set the Scene:** Arrange a circle with candles, decorations, and a central altar or Yule log.
2. **Invite Participants:** Encourage each person to bring a small token or written blessing to contribute to the circle.
3. **Exchange Blessings:** Go around the circle, allowing each person to share a blessing or gratitude. Add their tokens to the altar or Yule log.
4. **Group Intention:** Close the circle with a collective intention or prayer, such as:
   "May our blessings flow freely into the world, bringing light and joy to all who need it."

2. Creating and Distributing Blessing Bags

Blessing bags are small bundles of love and care that can be given to friends, family, or those in need.

Contents for Blessing Bags:

- Herbal sachets (lavender for peace, rosemary for protection)
- Crystals (amethyst for calm, citrine for abundance)
- Candles or small tokens of light
- Handwritten notes or affirmations

Distribute these bags to loved ones, neighbors, or local shelters as a way to share the spirit of Yule.

3. Volunteering and Acts of Kindness

Share your blessings by giving your time and energy to your community:

- Volunteer at a local food bank, shelter, or community center.
- Organize a donation drive for winter clothing, blankets, or food.
- Perform random acts of kindness, such as paying for someone's coffee, shoveling a neighbor's driveway, or leaving anonymous notes of encouragement.

4. Hosting a Yule Feast for Sharing

Invite friends, family, or neighbors to a Yule-themed gathering, emphasizing community and gratitude.

- Prepare traditional Yule foods and drinks, incorporating seasonal ingredients.
- Share blessings around the table, with each guest expressing something they are thankful for.
- Offer small take-home tokens, such as handmade ornaments or candles, to spread the energy of the season.

The Power of Blessings and Gratitude

Expressing gratitude and sharing blessings during Yule creates a flow of positive energy that enriches both your life and the lives of those around you. Gratitude amplifies abundance, strengthens connections, and aligns you with the cycles of nature, reminding you of the infinite blessings present even in the darkest times.

By performing rituals to honor your blessings and extending them to your community, you embody the true spirit of Yule—one of light, renewal, and love. Let your acts of gratitude and generosity be a beacon of hope and joy, illuminating the path forward as the Sun returns.

Chapter 17: Creating Yule Traditions

Yule, the Winter Solstice, is a season of light, renewal, and connection. It provides the perfect opportunity to craft personal and family traditions that honor both the past and present while laying the groundwork for future celebrations. By incorporating meaningful rituals, magical practices, and elements of creativity, you can design a unique Yule experience that becomes a cherished part of your spiritual and familial legacy.

This chapter explores how to craft personal and family traditions for Yule and offers guidance on passing down magical practices to future generations, ensuring the spirit of Yule lives on.

Crafting Personal and Family Traditions for a Unique Yule Experience

Creating Yule traditions is about more than following ancient customs—it's about infusing the season with practices that resonate with your values, beliefs, and lifestyle. By blending the old with the new, you create a celebration that is uniquely yours.

1. Establishing a Yule Morning Ritual

A special morning ritual can set the tone for the day and create a sense of magic and renewal:

- Begin the day by lighting a candle and welcoming the Sun's return, saying:
  "With this light, I honor the rebirth of the Sun and the blessings it brings."
- Share warm drinks like spiced cider or herbal tea while reflecting on intentions for the coming year.
- Encourage each family member to write a wish or goal on a piece of paper to place on the Yule altar or bury beneath a tree.

2. Decorating with Intention

Transform decorating into a ritual by infusing your space with magical energy:

- **The Yule Tree:**
    - Decorate with ornaments that symbolize protection, abundance, and renewal, such as stars, suns, and evergreen sprigs.
    - Add handmade charms or wishes written on paper ornaments.
    - Light the tree with candles or eco-friendly lights, symbolizing the returning light of the Sun.
- **Seasonal Altars:**
    - Create a Yule altar with candles, crystals, and natural elements like pinecones and holly.
    - Include personal items or symbols of gratitude to honor the past year.

3. Crafting Family Keepsakes

Create items that can be used year after year, becoming symbols of your family's Yule traditions:

- **A Family Yule Log:** Decorate a special log each year, burning it in the hearth or keeping it as a centerpiece.
- **Yule Ornaments:** Make handmade ornaments with meaningful symbols, dates, or family initials.
- **Blessing Books:** Start a journal where family members write blessings, wishes, or reflections each Yule.

4. Incorporating Seasonal Foods and Feasts

Shared meals are central to Yule celebrations, providing nourishment for both body and spirit:

- Prepare traditional Yule dishes like roasted meats, spiced cakes, or mulled wine.
- Host a "Blessing Feast" where each dish represents a theme (e.g., abundance, love, or renewal).
- Include a gratitude moment where each person shares something they're thankful for before the meal begins.

5. Community-Centered Traditions

Bring the spirit of Yule into your community by:

- Hosting a Yule gathering or open house with neighbors and friends.
- Sharing baked goods or handmade ornaments as blessings for others.
- Organizing a group ritual or candlelight walk to honor the Solstice.

6. Aligning with Nature

Nature is at the heart of Yule. Build traditions that honor the Earth's cycles:

- **Winter Walks:** Take a family walk in nature to gather evergreen branches, pinecones, or other natural decorations.
- **Tree Blessings:** Visit a nearby tree to leave offerings of birdseed or biodegradable ornaments, expressing gratitude for its presence.
- **Star Watching:** On Solstice night, spend time under the stars, reflecting on the vastness of the universe and your connection to it.

Passing Down Magical Practices to Future Generations

Yule is an opportunity to instill a sense of wonder, connection, and magic in younger generations. By sharing meaningful practices, you create a foundation for lifelong spiritual exploration.

1. Teaching the Meaning of Yule

Help children or new practitioners understand the significance of Yule:

- Share the story of the Sun's rebirth, using simple language or visual aids like a storytelling board.
- Explain the symbolism of common Yule elements (e.g., evergreens for eternal life, candles for light).
- Create age-appropriate rituals, such as lighting candles, making wishes, or decorating with natural items.

2. Making Magic Accessible

Involve children or newcomers in magical practices that are simple yet meaningful:

- **Charm Crafting:** Teach them how to make protective or luck charms using herbs, beads, or ribbons.
- **Seasonal Baking:** Add a magical element to baking by stirring intentions into the batter or decorating cookies with symbols.
- **Candle Magic:** Guide them in lighting a candle for a specific intention, such as gratitude or hope.

3. Creating Family Rituals

Develop rituals that can be performed together, fostering connection and continuity:

- **The Wishing Flame:** Have each person light a small candle, making a wish or setting an intention for the coming year. Combine the candles into a single flame to symbolize unity.
- **Storytelling Circles:** Share stories about ancestors, past Yule celebrations, or personal reflections to honor family history.
- **Seasonal Crafting:** Work together to create Yule decorations, ornaments, or gifts infused with love and intention.

4. Keeping Traditions Flexible

As families grow and change, traditions should evolve to remain meaningful:

- Allow each family member to suggest new elements or activities to incorporate into Yule celebrations.
- Adapt rituals to accommodate different spiritual paths, ensuring inclusivity and respect.
- Embrace spontaneity, allowing space for organic moments of joy and connection.

5. Building a Legacy

Ensure your Yule traditions endure by creating a tangible legacy:

- Write down rituals, recipes, and stories in a family grimoire or Yule journal.
- Record your celebrations through photos, videos, or scrapbooks to preserve memories.
- Pass down symbolic items, such as a cherished Yule log, altar cloth, or special ornament.

Examples of Family Yule Traditions

Here are examples of traditions you can adopt or adapt to create a meaningful Yule experience:

- **Solstice Countdown:** Create an advent-style calendar leading up to Yule, with daily activities like lighting a candle, sharing gratitude, or performing a small act of kindness.
- **Yule Wish Tree:** Write wishes or intentions on small ornaments and hang them on the tree, leaving them up until the New Year.
- **Midnight Sun Walk:** On Solstice night, take a quiet walk under the stars, reflecting on the year's blessings and setting intentions for the future.
- **Yule Storybook:** Create a book with seasonal stories, myths, and memories to be read aloud each year.

The Joy of Tradition

Creating Yule traditions is a magical process that brings meaning, connection, and joy to the season. These practices serve as anchors in an ever-changing world, offering a sense of continuity and belonging. By crafting traditions that reflect your values and sharing them with future generations, you ensure that the light of Yule continues to shine brightly, year after year.

Let your traditions become a source of inspiration, love, and renewal, embodying the true spirit of Yule and passing its magic down through the ages.

Chapter 18: Winter Solstice Meditation

The Winter Solstice, the longest night of the year, is a time of reflection, renewal, and alignment with the rhythms of nature. Meditation during Yule connects you to the transformative energy of the season, fostering inner calm and clarity as you prepare for the returning light. This chapter offers a detailed guided meditation to align with the Solstice's energy and provides tips for finding peace and insight during this sacred time.

Guided Meditation to Align with the Energy of the Solstice

Meditation allows you to immerse yourself in the energy of the Winter Solstice, embracing both the stillness of the long night and the hope of the returning light. This guided practice focuses on grounding, releasing the old, and welcoming renewal.

Preparation for Meditation

Before beginning your meditation, take a few steps to create a sacred and comfortable space:

1. **Choose a Quiet Setting:** Find a space where you won't be disturbed. Dim the lights or use candles to create a serene atmosphere.
2. **Gather Symbolic Items:** Enhance your meditation with seasonal elements, such as:
    - A gold or white candle to symbolize the Sun's return.
    - Evergreen branches for renewal.
    - A small crystal, such as clear quartz (clarity) or amethyst (calmness).
3. **Wear Comfortable Clothing:** Choose warm, loose-fitting clothes to help you relax.
4. **Optional Soundscape:** Play soft instrumental music, nature sounds, or Solstice-themed chants to support your focus.

The Guided Meditation

This meditation is structured to help you align with the Solstice energy in three stages: grounding, releasing, and welcoming renewal.

1. Grounding in the Darkness

- Sit comfortably with your back straight and your feet flat on the ground or cross-legged. Rest your hands gently on your knees or in your lap.
- Close your eyes and take three deep breaths, inhaling through your nose and exhaling through your mouth. Feel the breath filling your body, grounding you in the present moment.
- Imagine roots growing from the base of your spine or the soles of your feet, extending deep into the Earth. Feel the solid, nurturing energy of the Earth supporting you, grounding you in its stability and strength.
- Say silently or aloud:
  "I am grounded, connected to the Earth, and supported by its energy."

2. Reflecting and Releasing the Old

- As you continue to breathe deeply, picture yourself standing in a vast winter landscape under a starry sky. The air is crisp, and the ground beneath you is covered in snow, symbolizing purity and renewal.
- Reflect on the past year. Allow memories, emotions, and challenges to arise without judgment.
- Imagine holding a small bundle of these thoughts and feelings in your hands. This bundle represents what you are ready to release—fears, doubts, or patterns that no longer serve you.

- Visualize a warm light glowing within your chest, spreading to your hands and dissolving the bundle. Feel the weight lifting from your spirit as you let go of what no longer serves you.
- Say silently or aloud:
"I release what is no longer needed. I make space for new light and growth."

3. Welcoming the Light and Renewal

- Shift your focus to the horizon in your mind's eye. Imagine the first rays of the Solstice Sun rising, spreading golden light across the landscape. Feel the warmth of the light touching your skin, entering your heart, and filling your entire being with hope and vitality.
- Visualize this light illuminating your path for the coming year. See yourself moving forward with clarity, strength, and purpose.
- Hold an intention or affirmation in your mind, such as:
"I welcome the light into my life. I am renewed, and my path is clear."
- Take a few moments to bask in this energy, feeling gratitude for the light, the Earth, and the cycles of renewal.

4. Returning to the Present

- Gradually bring your awareness back to your physical surroundings. Wiggle your fingers and toes, and gently stretch if needed.
- When you're ready, open your eyes. Take a deep breath and carry the calm, centered energy of the meditation with you into your day.

Finding Inner Calm and Clarity during Yule

The Solstice provides a unique opportunity to embrace stillness and reconnect with your inner self. Incorporating meditation and mindfulness into your Yule celebrations helps you maintain balance, clarity, and peace during the busy holiday season.

1. Incorporating Mindfulness into Daily Life

You don't need a formal meditation to benefit from the Solstice's energy. Simple mindfulness practices can help you stay centered:

- **Morning Rituals:** Light a candle each morning and spend a moment reflecting on your intentions for the day.
- **Mindful Walks:** Take a walk in nature, focusing on the sights, sounds, and sensations around you.
- **Gratitude Practice:** At the end of each day, write down three things you are grateful for, aligning with the season's themes of abundance and renewal.

2. Meditating with Seasonal Symbols

Using Yule-themed objects in your meditation enhances your connection to the season:

- **Candles:** Gaze at the flame of a candle to focus your mind and connect with the returning light.
- **Evergreens:** Hold or place a sprig of evergreen nearby to symbolize resilience and renewal.
- **Crystals:** Meditate with crystals like citrine (joy and abundance), clear quartz (clarity), or garnet (strength and grounding).

3. Creating a Solstice Altar for Meditation

An altar can serve as a focal point for your meditation practice:

- **Decorate with Seasonal Elements:** Include items like evergreen branches, pinecones, candles, and Sun symbols.
- **Add Personal Touches:** Incorporate objects that hold meaning for you, such as photos, letters, or charms.
- **Use the Altar Daily:** Sit before your altar for a few moments each day during Yule, meditating or reflecting on its symbols.

4. Journaling for Clarity

Pair meditation with journaling to deepen your insights:

- After meditating, write down any thoughts, emotions, or images that arose.
- Reflect on how these relate to your current path and the intentions you wish to set for the new year.
- Use prompts like:
    - *What am I ready to release as the year ends?*
    - *What new light do I wish to welcome into my life?*
    - *How can I align more closely with my true purpose?*

The Transformative Power of Solstice Meditation

Winter Solstice meditation is more than a practice—it's a journey into the heart of the season's energy. By embracing the darkness, releasing the old, and welcoming the light, you align with the cycles of nature and your own inner transformation.

As you meditate during Yule, allow yourself to find peace in stillness, clarity in reflection, and hope in the promise of renewal. Let the light of the Solstice guide you into a new year filled with purpose, growth, and harmony.

Chapter 19: The Spirit of Giving

Yule is a time of generosity and connection, reflecting the natural cycle of giving and receiving that sustains life. The return of the Sun symbolizes abundance and renewal, encouraging us to share our light with others. Giving during the Yule season is not just about material gifts—it's about offering love, kindness, and support, and doing so with magical intent. Likewise, receiving with gratitude completes the energetic exchange, fostering balance and harmony.

This chapter explores magical approaches to giving and receiving during Yule and offers guidance on gifting from the heart and sharing your abundance in meaningful ways.

Magical Approaches to Giving and Receiving during the Yule Season

Gift-giving at Yule can be a deeply spiritual act, imbued with intention and magic. By viewing gifts as symbols of connection and energy, you transform this seasonal tradition into a practice that honors the cycles of nature and strengthens bonds.

1. The Magic of Intentional Giving

Intentional giving focuses on the thought and energy behind the gift rather than its material value.

Steps for Magical Giving:

- **Set an Intention:** Before choosing a gift, think about what you want the recipient to feel or experience. For example:
  - *Love and comfort.*
  - *Renewal and growth.*
  - *Protection and support.*
- **Infuse the Gift with Energy:** As you wrap the gift, hold it in your hands and visualize it glowing with light. Imagine your intention infusing the object with energy, creating a magical connection.

- **Add a Personal Touch:** Include a handwritten note, a charm, or a small token that reflects the recipient's personality or your shared bond.

2. Ritualized Gift Exchanges

Enhance the act of giving by incorporating simple rituals:

- **Cleansing the Gift:** Pass the gift through incense smoke or sprinkle it with salt water to purify its energy.
- **Blessing the Exchange:** Before giving the gift, say:
  "With this offering, I share my light. May it bring joy, love, and blessings bright."
- **Expressing Gratitude:** When receiving a gift, take a moment to thank the giver sincerely and acknowledge the energy behind the gift.

3. Balancing Giving and Receiving

The energy of Yule is about balance—between light and darkness, action and rest, giving and receiving. To honor this balance:

- **Practice Gratitude:** Whether you are giving or receiving, approach the exchange with a sense of appreciation.
- **Give Thoughtfully:** Avoid over-giving to the point of depletion. Instead, focus on meaningful gestures that align with your values.
- **Receive Gracefully:** Accept gifts with an open heart, recognizing them as symbols of connection and care.

How to Gift from the Heart and Share Your Abundance

The most meaningful gifts are those that come from the heart, reflecting the spirit of love, gratitude, and abundance. Yule provides an opportunity to give in ways that uplift others and deepen your connection to the season's energy.

1. Crafting Handmade Gifts

Handmade gifts carry the unique energy of the giver, making them powerful symbols of love and intention.

Ideas for Handmade Yule Gifts:

- **Charm Bags:** Create small pouches filled with herbs, crystals, or tokens aligned with the recipient's needs (e.g., lavender for calm, citrine for abundance).
- **Decorative Ornaments:** Craft Yule-themed ornaments using natural materials like pinecones, wood, or dried fruit.
- **Personalized Candles:** Decorate or anoint candles with oils and herbs to create gifts for protection, love, or renewal.
- **Baked Goods:** Infuse your baking with magical intent by stirring love or prosperity into the dough.

As you create, focus on your intention for the recipient, imbuing the gift with positive energy.

2. Sharing Acts of Kindness

Giving doesn't always require a physical gift. Acts of kindness can be just as meaningful, especially during the Yule season:

- **Offer Your Time:** Help a friend or neighbor with a task, such as decorating, cooking, or running errands.
- **Provide Comfort:** Visit someone who may be feeling lonely or bring a warm meal to someone in need.

- **Create Joy:** Write heartfelt letters or leave anonymous notes of encouragement in public places.

These gestures spread the spirit of Yule far and wide, creating ripples of positivity.

3. Donating and Supporting Your Community

The Yule season is a time to recognize your abundance and share it with those who may be struggling.

Ways to Give Back:

- **Donate Warm Clothing and Blankets:** Collect and donate items to shelters to help those in need during the cold months.
- **Support Local Charities:** Offer financial contributions, volunteer your time, or participate in community food drives.
- **Gift to Nature:** Plant trees, feed birds, or clean up outdoor spaces to give back to the Earth.

4. Hosting a Giving Circle

A giving circle is a communal event where participants exchange gifts or blessings in a spirit of mutual support and connection.

How to Host a Giving Circle:

1. Invite friends, family, or members of your spiritual community.
2. Set an intention for the gathering, such as sharing abundance, expressing gratitude, or spreading joy.
3. Encourage each participant to bring a small, meaningful gift, such as a handmade item, a written blessing, or a token of nature.
4. Create a ritual to exchange the gifts, such as passing them around a circle while sharing words of gratitude or intention.

5. Aligning Your Giving with Yule's Themes

Each gift can reflect the spirit of Yule and its themes of renewal, connection, and light:

- **For Renewal:** Give seeds, plants, or journals to inspire growth and transformation.
- **For Connection:** Share gifts that encourage togetherness, such as games, books, or shared experiences.
- **For Light:** Offer candles, crystals, or Sun-themed items to symbolize the returning light of the Solstice.

6. Creating a Gratitude Ritual

Balance the act of giving by creating space to express gratitude for your own blessings. A simple ritual might include:

- Lighting a candle and reflecting on what you've received over the past year.
- Writing down five things you are grateful for and placing the list on your Yule altar.
- Saying:
  "As I give, so I receive. With gratitude, I honor the abundance in my life."

The Joy of Giving and Receiving

The spirit of giving during Yule is not about material wealth but about creating connections, sharing light, and honoring the flow of abundance. By giving with intention and receiving with gratitude, you align with the season's energy and strengthen the bonds between yourself, your community, and the world around you.

As you exchange gifts, perform acts of kindness, or share your time, remember that every gesture—no matter how small—carries the potential to brighten someone's life. In this way, the spirit of giving becomes a reflection of the Sun's return, spreading warmth, hope, and renewal to all.

Chapter 20: Yule Symbolism in Daily Life

Yule, the Winter Solstice, is rich with symbols that represent light, renewal, and the cycles of nature. These symbols are not only meaningful during the holiday season but can also be integrated into your daily magical practice to strengthen your connection to Yule's energies year-round. By weaving these powerful symbols into your life, you align with the themes of hope, growth, and balance, fostering a deeper spiritual connection.

This chapter explores how to incorporate Yule symbols into your everyday practice and offers ways to sustain your connection to Yule's energies beyond the season.

Integrating Yule Symbols into Your Daily Magical Practice

Yule symbols, such as evergreens, candles, and stars, carry potent energies that resonate with the Solstice's themes. Incorporating these symbols into your daily life enhances your spiritual practice, bringing the magic of Yule into every moment.

1. The Symbolism of Yule Elements

Each Yule symbol holds specific meanings and energies that can support your intentions:

- **Evergreens:** Represent resilience, eternal life, and protection.
- **Candles and Fire:** Symbolize the returning light, transformation, and spiritual illumination.
- **Holly and Ivy:** Reflect balance, renewal, and the interconnectedness of life.
- **The Sun:** Represents hope, vitality, and the cyclical nature of time.

- **Stars:** Signify guidance, inspiration, and the vastness of the cosmos.

By understanding the meanings of these symbols, you can use them intentionally in your magical practices.

2. Using Yule Symbols in Your Altar Space

Your altar is a sacred place for focusing your energy and intentions. Decorate it with Yule symbols to keep their magic alive:

- **Evergreen Branches:** Place fresh or dried evergreen sprigs on your altar to invoke resilience and renewal.
- **Candles:** Use white, gold, or green candles to represent light and growth.
- **Holly and Berries:** Arrange holly sprigs around your altar for protection and balance.
- **Sun Symbols:** Include items like golden ornaments, solar images, or handmade Sun charms to honor the light.
- **Crystals:** Incorporate crystals such as citrine (abundance), garnet (strength), and clear quartz (clarity).

Refresh your altar regularly, rotating symbols and decorations to reflect your current intentions and seasonal cycles.

3. Incorporating Yule Energies into Daily Rituals

Small, intentional actions can help you channel Yule's energies throughout the year:

- **Morning Candle Lighting:** Begin each day by lighting a candle and focusing on an affirmation, such as:
  "With this light, I welcome clarity and renewal into my life."
- **Gratitude Practice:** Use a small evergreen token or Sun charm to hold as you express gratitude for the blessings in your life.

- **Daily Offerings:** Place offerings like water, herbs, or seeds on your altar to honor the cycles of nature and the abundance around you.

4. Symbols in Meditation and Visualization

Use Yule symbols to enhance your meditation practice:

- **Evergreens:** Visualize yourself standing among evergreen trees, absorbing their strength and resilience.
- **The Sun:** Picture the rising Sun illuminating your path, filling you with warmth and vitality.
- **Stars:** Meditate on a star to focus on your goals and dreams, imagining its light guiding you forward.

These visualizations align your energy with Yule's themes, fostering balance and hope.

Strengthening Your Connection to Yule Energies Year-Round

While Yule is a seasonal celebration, its energies of light, renewal, and transformation can guide you throughout the year. By maintaining a connection to these energies, you stay grounded in the rhythms of nature and aligned with your spiritual goals.

1. Living in Harmony with the Seasons

Yule is part of the larger Wheel of the Year, which reflects the natural cycles of growth, harvest, rest, and renewal. Strengthen your connection to Yule by embracing seasonal living:

- **Winter (Yule):** Focus on rest, reflection, and planning.
- **Spring:** Act on the intentions set during Yule, planting seeds for growth.
- **Summer:** Celebrate achievements and embrace vitality.
- **Autumn:** Harvest the results of your efforts and prepare for introspection.

By honoring each season, you maintain a continuous connection to Yule's transformative energy.

2. Creating Year-Round Rituals Inspired by Yule

Design rituals that keep Yule's magic alive throughout the year:

- **Monthly Candle Rituals:** On the full or new moon, light a candle to reconnect with the returning light and your intentions.
- **Seasonal Gratitude Practice:** Reflect on your blessings at the turn of each season, using Yule symbols like holly or evergreens as a focal point.
- **Personal Renewal Rituals:** Periodically review your goals and release what no longer serves you, just as you did during the Solstice.

3. Carrying Yule Symbols with You

Keep small Yule symbols on hand as daily reminders of the Solstice's energy:

- **Evergreen Sprigs:** Place a small sprig in your wallet, bag, or desk for protection and resilience.
- **Sun Charms:** Wear or carry a Sun charm to embody hope and vitality.
- **Crystal Talismans:** Carry a pocket-sized citrine or garnet to channel abundance and strength.

These items act as anchors, keeping you aligned with Yule's themes wherever you go.

4. Infusing Your Home with Yule Energies

Transform your living space into a sanctuary that reflects Yule's magic:

- **Decorate with Evergreen Wreaths:** Keep evergreen wreaths or garlands in your home to symbolize eternal life.
- **Use Seasonal Colors:** Incorporate Yule's traditional colors—green, gold, and white—into your decor.
- **Light Seasonal Candles:** Burn candles with seasonal scents like pine, cinnamon, or frankincense to evoke Yule's warmth.

These small touches create a nurturing environment that supports your spiritual practice.

5. Reflecting on Yule's Lessons

Yule teaches us to embrace the cycles of light and darkness, growth and rest. Regular reflection on these lessons can deepen your connection to its energy:

- **Journaling Prompts:**
  - *What light am I nurturing within myself?*
  - *What lessons have I learned from times of darkness?*
  - *How can I honor the cycles of nature in my daily life?*
- **Meditation Questions:**
  - *How does the balance of light and dark appear in my life?*
  - *What areas of my life need renewal or release?*

Sustaining the Spirit of Yule

Integrating Yule symbols and energies into your daily life allows you to live in harmony with the cycles of nature and stay connected to your spiritual path. Whether through simple rituals, meaningful symbols, or ongoing reflections, Yule's magic becomes a guiding light, offering strength and inspiration throughout the year.

By embracing Yule's themes—light, renewal, and balance—you create a life infused with purpose, gratitude, and connection. Let the symbols of Yule serve as daily reminders of your inner power and the infinite cycles of transformation that guide us all.

Chapter 21: Yule for Solitary Practitioners

Yule, the Winter Solstice, is a deeply personal time for reflection, renewal, and honoring the cycles of nature. For solitary practitioners, celebrating Yule alone can be profoundly meaningful, offering an opportunity to create personalized rituals and connect intimately with the energies of the season. By aligning your practices with the themes of light, transformation, and gratitude, you can experience the magic of Yule in a way that feels uniquely your own.

This chapter explores how to celebrate a meaningful Yule as a solitary practitioner and provides guidance for creating personal rituals to honor the Winter Solstice.

How to Celebrate a Meaningful Yule Alone

Celebrating Yule alone allows you to focus inward, embracing the season's transformative energy without distraction. Solitary practices emphasize introspection, intention-setting, and connection to nature and spirit.

1. Setting the Tone for Your Celebration

Create an atmosphere that aligns with the spirit of Yule:

- **Decorate Your Space:** Incorporate Yule symbols such as candles, evergreens, holly, and Sun imagery.
- **Use Seasonal Scents:** Burn incense or diffuse essential oils like pine, frankincense, or cinnamon to evoke the energy of the season.
- **Prepare a Yule Altar:** Arrange items that symbolize the Solstice, such as crystals (citrine, garnet), a Sun-shaped ornament, and a small candle to represent the returning light.

2. Reflecting on the Year Past

Yule is a time for closure and renewal. Spend time reflecting on the past year:

- **Journaling Prompts:** Write about your accomplishments, challenges, and lessons learned. Consider:
    - *What am I proud of this year?*
    - *What do I wish to release as the year ends?*
    - *What new light do I want to welcome into my life?*
- **Create a Gratitude List:** Write down things you're grateful for and place the list on your altar as an offering to the season.

3. Watching the Sunrise or Sunset

The Winter Solstice is the shortest day and longest night of the year, making the Sun's journey especially significant.

- **Sunrise Ritual:** Rise early and watch the Sun as it begins to climb the horizon. Offer a simple prayer or affirmation, such as: *"I honor the rebirth of the Sun, the light that guides me, and the warmth that sustains me."*
- **Sunset Reflection:** Watch the Sun set, symbolizing the cycle of release and renewal. Reflect on what you wish to leave behind in the darkness and what you welcome into the light.

4. Preparing a Solitary Feast

Even alone, a special meal can be a sacred and magical act:

- **Seasonal Foods:** Prepare dishes that align with Yule's themes, such as spiced cakes, roasted vegetables, and warm cider.
- **Bless Your Food:** Before eating, take a moment to bless the meal, expressing gratitude for the nourishment it provides.

- **Set an Intention:** As you eat, focus on the energy of renewal and abundance that you are inviting into your life.

5. Solitary Rituals for Yule

Personal rituals are powerful tools for connecting with the energies of Yule.

Creating Personal Rituals to Honor the Winter Solstice

Designing rituals that resonate with your beliefs and practices allows you to celebrate Yule in a way that feels deeply authentic. Below are ideas for solitary Yule rituals.

1. The Candle Ritual of Light

This ritual symbolizes the return of the Sun and invites light into your life.

Materials Needed:

- A gold or white candle (for light and renewal)
- A piece of paper and pen
- A small bowl of water or salt

Steps:

1. **Prepare Your Space:** Cleanse your area with incense or sound to create a sacred atmosphere.
2. **Set Your Intention:** Write down an intention or affirmation for the coming year, such as:
   "I welcome clarity, abundance, and joy into my life."
3. **Light the Candle:** Say:
   "On this longest night, I light this flame to honor the returning Sun. May its light guide my path and fill my life with warmth and hope."
4. **Focus on the Flame:** Meditate on the candlelight, visualizing it illuminating your life and dispelling any darkness or doubt.
5. **Seal the Intention:** Place your written intention under the candle or in a special box on your altar.

2. Releasing the Old with a Fire Ritual

This ritual helps you release what no longer serves you, making space for renewal.

Materials Needed:

- A small, safe fire source (firepit, fireplace, or heatproof dish for burning paper)
- A piece of paper and pen

Steps:

1. **Reflect:** Write down anything you wish to release—habits, fears, or challenges from the past year.
2. **Create Sacred Space:** Light a candle or incense and sit quietly, focusing on your breath.
3. **Burn the Paper:** Safely burn the paper, saying:
   "As this burns, I release what no longer serves me. I am free to grow and thrive."
4. **Offer Gratitude:** Thank the fire for its transformative energy and visualize yourself lighter and more open to new possibilities.

3. A Meditation on the Turning Wheel

This meditation connects you to the cycles of nature and your place within them.

Steps:

1. Sit comfortably and close your eyes. Take a few deep breaths, grounding yourself in the present moment.
2. Visualize a great wheel turning slowly. Each spoke represents a season, and the wheel's movement reflects the passage of time.
3. See yourself standing at the Winter Solstice, the wheel's point of stillness. Feel the balance of light and dark, rest and renewal.

4. Imagine the wheel beginning to turn again, carrying you forward into a new cycle. Reflect on what you wish to bring into this next phase of your journey.

5. End the meditation by saying:
   "I honor the turning wheel of life. I am part of its endless cycles, renewed and ready for what is to come."

4. Creating a Personal Yule Charm

Crafting a charm to carry Yule's energy with you can serve as a year-round reminder of the Solstice's lessons.

Materials Needed:

- A small pouch or piece of cloth
- Herbs (such as cinnamon, rosemary, or pine)
- A crystal (such as citrine or garnet)
- A small Sun or star charm

Steps:

1. Combine the herbs and crystal in the pouch, focusing on your intention (e.g., renewal, protection, abundance).
2. Add the charm, visualizing it glowing with light and energy.
3. Seal the pouch and hold it in your hands, saying:
   "With this charm, I carry the light of Yule. May it guide and protect me throughout the year."
4. Keep the charm on your altar, in your pocket, or under your pillow.

Sustaining Yule's Magic

Celebrating Yule as a solitary practitioner is an opportunity to deepen your connection to yourself, nature, and the cycles of life. By creating personal rituals and integrating Yule's symbols and themes into your daily life, you carry the magic of the Winter Solstice with you long after the season has passed.

Let Yule remind you that even in the darkest times, the light returns, bringing renewal, hope, and endless possibilities. Through intentional practice, you honor both the outer cycles of nature and the inner transformations of your spirit, aligning with the timeless magic of the Solstice.

Chapter 22: The Role of Divination in Yule

Yule, the Winter Solstice, is a time of deep introspection and renewal, making it an ideal season for divination. The longest night of the year invites you to look inward, seek guidance, and align with the cycles of nature to prepare for the coming year. Whether you use tarot, runes, pendulums, or other tools, divination during Yule can reveal insights about the past, illuminate your path forward, and help you set meaningful intentions.

This chapter explores how to use divination tools for Yule guidance and provides detailed rituals for predicting and preparing for the year ahead.

Using Tarot, Runes, and Other Tools for Yule Guidance

Divination tools serve as mirrors for your subconscious and conduits for connecting with universal energies. During Yule, they can help you uncover hidden truths, clarify intentions, and align your actions with the natural cycles of light and darkness.

1. Tarot for Yule

Tarot is a versatile tool for exploring your journey and gaining insight into the energies surrounding the Solstice.

Suggested Yule Tarot Spreads:

- **The Solstice Light Spread (5 Cards):**
  This spread helps you reflect on the past year and prepare for the light's return.
  1. *The Longest Night:* What challenges have you faced this year?
  2. *The Returning Light:* What energy is beginning to grow in your life?
  3. *Illuminating the Path:* What guidance do you need for the coming year?
  4. *Hidden Lessons:* What lessons from the past year should you carry forward?
  5. *Your Inner Flame:* What will inspire and sustain you in the year ahead?
- **Wheel of the Year Spread (12 Cards):**
  Draw one card for each month to reveal the energies and themes that will shape your year.

Enhancing Your Tarot Practice:

- Use candles, crystals, or herbs (like rosemary or frankincense) to cleanse your deck and create a sacred space.

- Journal your interpretations to track patterns and reflect on your growth over time.

2. Runes for Yule

Runes are an ancient divination tool associated with Norse and Germanic traditions, making them particularly aligned with Yule's themes of wisdom and cycles.

Yule Rune Ritual:

1. **Preparation:** Cleanse your rune set with smoke or place them in moonlight overnight.
2. **Drawing a Rune:** Hold the rune bag in your hands, focusing on a question or intention for the coming year. Draw one rune and interpret its message.
   - For example:
     - *Fehu* (wealth): Abundance and new opportunities await.
     - *Dagaz* (day): Transformation and light are on the horizon.
     - *Isa* (ice): Pause and reflect before taking action.
3. **Reflection:** Journal your insights and consider how the rune's meaning applies to your current situation or goals.

Rune Casting Spread for Yule:

- Cast three runes onto a cloth or table:
  1. *The Past Year:* What lessons have shaped you?
  2. *The Present Moment:* What energy surrounds you now?
  3. *The Coming Year:* What guidance will support your path forward?

3. Pendulum Divination for Yule

Pendulums are simple yet effective tools for asking yes/no questions or exploring specific areas of focus.

Yule Pendulum Ritual:

- **Setting Intentions:** Hold your pendulum and state your intention for clarity and truth.
- **Questions for Yule:**
    - *Am I aligned with the energy of renewal?*
    - *Is this the right time to pursue a particular goal?*
    - *What should I focus on to manifest abundance in the coming year?*
- **Directional Guidance:** Use a pendulum board or create one with quadrants labeled "Love," "Health," "Career," and "Spirituality" to identify areas needing attention.

4. Other Divination Tools for Yule

- **Scrying:** Use a black mirror, bowl of water, or candle flame to access visions and insights during meditation.
- **Oracle Cards:** These cards offer thematic guidance and can complement other divination methods.
- **Astrology:** Reflect on planetary alignments during the Solstice to understand the collective energies influencing your life.

Rituals to Predict and Prepare for the Coming Year

Divination rituals during Yule focus on releasing the old, setting intentions, and seeking guidance for the future. These practices align your energy with the transformative power of the Solstice.

1. The Solstice Divination Ritual

This ritual combines candle magic and divination to create a sacred moment of insight and renewal.

Materials Needed:

- A white or gold candle (for clarity and light)
- Your preferred divination tool (tarot, runes, pendulum, etc.)
- A journal or notepad

Steps:

1. **Cleanse the Space:** Use incense or sound to purify your space and focus your mind.
2. **Light the Candle:** Say:
   "On this longest night, I seek wisdom and light. May clarity and truth guide my path."
3. **Perform Divination:** Use your chosen tool to explore the energies of the coming year. Ask questions such as:
   - *What do I need to release as the year ends?*
   - *What opportunities will the new year bring?*
   - *How can I align with my highest purpose?*
4. **Record Insights:** Write down your findings and reflect on how they align with your intentions.
5. **Close the Ritual:** Extinguish the candle with gratitude, saying:
   "With this light, I welcome renewal and wisdom into my life."

2. The Yule Dreaming Ritual

Dreams are a powerful source of guidance and inspiration, especially during the Solstice.

Materials Needed:

- A small pouch or charm bag
- Herbs such as mugwort, chamomile, or lavender (to enhance dreaming)
- A clear quartz crystal

Steps:

1. **Create a Dream Pouch:** Combine the herbs and crystal in the pouch. Hold it in your hands and say:
   "As I sleep, may my dreams reveal the wisdom I seek."
2. **Place the Pouch:** Tuck the pouch under your pillow or near your bed.
3. **Set an Intention:** Before sleeping, focus on a specific question or area of guidance you wish to explore.
4. **Record Your Dreams:** Keep a journal nearby to write down your dreams upon waking. Reflect on any symbols or messages that arise.

3. Yearly Planning with Divination

Use divination to create a roadmap for the coming year, aligning your goals with the energies revealed during your practice.

Steps:

1. Perform a 12-card tarot spread, a rune casting, or another divination method to identify key themes for each month.
2. Note down insights for each period, including advice for navigating challenges and opportunities.
3. Use this information to set realistic goals and plan actions that align with your spiritual journey.

Making Divination a Yule Tradition

Integrating divination into your Yule celebrations allows you to deepen your connection with the season and its energies:

- Perform a personal reading each year to reflect on your growth and set intentions.
- Share divination practices with friends or family, creating a group ritual of insight and connection.
- Keep a divination journal to track patterns, lessons, and progress over time.

Embracing the Magic of Divination

The Winter Solstice offers a powerful moment to pause, reflect, and seek guidance for the road ahead. Through divination, you tap into the wisdom of the universe, aligning your intentions with the natural cycles of light and darkness.

As you practice divination during Yule, allow its insights to illuminate your path, empower your choices, and deepen your connection to the magic within and around you. By predicting and preparing for the coming year, you honor the transformative energy of Yule and step confidently into the light of renewal.

Chapter 23: Creating a Yule Spell Book

A Yule spell book is a sacred collection of rituals, incantations, and magical practices that celebrate the energy of the Winter Solstice. It serves as a personal grimoire, capturing the essence of Yule's themes—love, peace, and prosperity—and preserving them for future use. By crafting a Yule spell book, you create a timeless resource that not only deepens your spiritual connection to the season but also empowers your practice throughout the year.

This chapter provides a comprehensive guide to collecting Yule-specific spells and outlines techniques for empowering your spell book to ensure its potency and longevity.

Collecting Yule-Specific Spells for Love, Peace, and Prosperity

Yule spells focus on renewal, harmony, and abundance, aligning with the transformative energy of the Solstice. When collecting spells for your Yule spell book, consider a variety of intentions that reflect your personal goals and the spirit of the season.

1. Spells for Love

Love spells during Yule focus on deepening existing bonds, fostering self-love, and attracting new connections.

Example: The Evergreen Heart Spell

Purpose: To strengthen love and connection.

Materials Needed:

- A sprig of evergreen (symbolizing eternal love).
- A pink or red candle (for love).
- A small piece of paper and a pen.

Instructions:

1. Write the name of your loved one (or "self-love" for personal intentions) on the paper.

2. Light the candle and hold the evergreen sprig over the flame (without burning it), saying:

"Evergreen, ever true, let love flourish and renew. With warmth and light, our hearts align, this love grows stronger, through space and time."

3. Place the paper and sprig on your altar or in a safe space to symbolize the growing bond.

2. Spells for Peace

Peace spells help you find inner calm, heal emotional wounds, and create harmony in your home.

Example: Winter Solstice Peace Candle Spell

Purpose: To bring tranquility and balance.

Materials Needed:

- A blue or white candle.
- Lavender or chamomile oil.
- A bowl of water.

Instructions:

1. Anoint the candle with lavender or chamomile oil, focusing on your intention for peace.
2. Light the candle and place the bowl of water in front of it.
3. Say:
   "On this Solstice night, I call for peace, Let chaos fade, and troubles cease. With water's calm and candle's light, I find my balance, my soul takes flight."
4. Meditate on the candlelight and water until you feel calm. Extinguish the candle and keep the bowl of water on your altar as a reminder of tranquility.

3. Spells for Prosperity

Prosperity spells during Yule align with the returning light and the abundance it promises.

Example: The Golden Sun Spell

Purpose: To attract wealth and opportunities.

Materials Needed:

- A gold candle (or yellow if gold is unavailable).
- A small coin or piece of gold-colored jewelry.
- Cinnamon powder or oil.

Instructions:

1. Anoint the candle with cinnamon oil or sprinkle cinnamon powder around its base.
2. Place the coin or jewelry near the candle as a representation of prosperity.
3. Light the candle and say:
   "Golden light, shining bright, draw abundance to my sight. Wealth and fortune, flow to me, as I will it, so mote it be."
4. Let the candle burn safely for a while, then extinguish it. Carry the coin or jewelry as a charm for continued abundance.

Empowering Your Spell Book for Future Use

Once you've collected your spells, it's important to empower your spell book to amplify its magical energy. Treating your spell book as a sacred object strengthens its connection to your practice.

1. Choosing and Preparing the Spell Book

Select a book that feels special and aligned with your intentions:

- **Options:** A blank journal, a leather-bound grimoire, or a digital document if you prefer technology.
- **Cleansing:** Before using the book, cleanse it with incense, moonlight, or salt to remove any residual energy.
- **Dedication:** Hold the book in your hands and say:
"I dedicate this book to the magic of Yule. May it hold the wisdom of the season and guide my path with light."

2. Organizing Your Spell Book

Structure your spell book for clarity and ease of use:

- **Sections by Intention:** Divide the book into categories like love, peace, prosperity, and general rituals.
- **Incorporate Symbols:** Add Yule-related drawings or symbols, such as evergreen branches, stars, or Sun motifs.
- **Personal Notes:** Leave space for reflections, results, and improvements to spells after use.

3. Empowering the Spell Book with Ritual

Perform a ritual to charge your spell book with magical energy:

Materials Needed:

- A white or gold candle.
- A piece of evergreen or holly.
- A clear quartz crystal.

Steps:

1. **Create Sacred Space:** Light the candle and place the evergreen and quartz on your altar.
2. **Focus Your Intentions:** Hold the book and visualize it glowing with golden light, filled with wisdom and power.
3. **Recite a Blessing:**
   "This book I charge with Yule's light, a sacred guide both day and night. Within these pages, magic flows, as above, so below."
4. **Seal the Energy:** Place the book on your altar with the evergreen and quartz overnight to absorb their energy.

4. Using Your Spell Book Throughout the Year

A Yule spell book is not just for the Solstice—it's a tool for year-round magic:

- **Seasonal Adaptations:** Modify Yule spells to align with other Sabbats or seasonal energies.
- **Regular Updates:** Add new spells, rituals, or reflections as your practice evolves.
- **Daily Inspiration:** Use the book as a source of guidance, selecting spells or affirmations to support your intentions.

Personalizing Your Yule Spell Book

Make your spell book a reflection of your unique practice:

- **Add Artwork:** Include drawings, pressed flowers, or printed images to enhance its beauty and meaning.
- **Incorporate Poetry:** Write or collect poems that inspire your connection to Yule.
- **Use Calligraphy:** Handwrite spells in elegant script to elevate their energy.

The Power of a Yule Spell Book

A Yule spell book is more than a collection of spells—it's a sacred repository of your magical journey. By gathering Yule-specific spells and empowering your book with intention and care, you create a tool that deepens your connection to the Solstice and enhances your practice throughout the year.

As you use and update your spell book, it becomes a living document, evolving with your spiritual path and holding the magic of your intentions. With every spell cast and every ritual recorded, your book becomes a testament to the light, love, and prosperity that Yule brings into your life.

Chapter 24: Ritual Baths and Self-Care

Yule, the Winter Solstice, is a time of reflection, renewal, and honoring the cycles of light and darkness. Amid the busyness of the holiday season, it's important to carve out time for personal care and spiritual renewal. Ritual baths and self-care practices provide powerful tools for cleansing the body, mind, and spirit, aligning you with the transformative energy of Yule. These practices help you stay grounded, balanced, and connected to the season's themes of renewal and light.

This chapter explores Yule-themed ritual baths for cleansing and renewal and offers self-care practices to help you stay centered during the holidays.

Yule-Themed Ritual Baths for Cleansing and Renewal

Ritual baths combine the healing power of water with magical ingredients and intention-setting. During Yule, these baths are ideal for releasing old energy, preparing for renewal, and aligning with the season's themes of light and warmth.

1. Preparing for a Ritual Bath

Creating a sacred atmosphere is key to the success of a ritual bath:

- **Cleanse Your Space:** Clean your bathroom and use incense, sage, or sound to purify the space.
- **Set the Mood:** Dim the lights, light candles, and play soft, soothing music to create a relaxing ambiance.
- **Gather Supplies:** Prepare magical ingredients, such as herbs, essential oils, crystals, and salts, aligned with your intentions.
- **Choose an Intention:** Focus on a specific goal, such as cleansing, renewal, or manifesting light.

2. Yule Ritual Bath Recipes

Here are three Yule-themed baths tailored to the season's energies:

The Evergreen Cleansing Bath

Purpose: To cleanse and release negative energy.

Ingredients:

- A handful of fresh or dried evergreen branches (pine, cedar, or fir).
- Epsom salt or sea salt.
- A few drops of rosemary essential oil (optional).

Steps:

1. Fill your tub with warm water and add the salt.
2. Place the evergreen branches in the water, focusing on their protective and cleansing properties.
3. As you soak, visualize the water washing away negativity and leaving you feeling refreshed and renewed.
4. Say:
   "With the strength of evergreens, I release the old, making space for renewal and light."

The Solstice Light Bath

Purpose: To invite warmth, light, and joy into your life.

Ingredients:

- Orange slices or peels (for solar energy).
- Cinnamon sticks (for warmth and abundance).
- A few drops of frankincense or citrus essential oil.
- Gold or yellow candles for ambiance.

Steps:

1. Add the orange slices and cinnamon sticks to your bathwater.
2. Light the candles and place them around the tub.
3. As you soak, visualize the light of the Solstice Sun filling your heart with warmth and hope.
4. Say:
   "As the Sun returns, so too does my light. I welcome joy, abundance, and love into my life."

The Winter Peace Bath

Purpose: To find inner calm and balance during the hectic holiday season.

Ingredients:

- Lavender and chamomile flowers (or essential oils).
- A handful of dried rose petals.
- Amethyst or clear quartz crystal (optional).

Steps:

1. Place the herbs in a muslin bag or directly into the bathwater.
2. Add the crystal to the water, if desired, to enhance calming energy.
3. Soak in the bath, breathing deeply and focusing on the stillness within.
4. Say:
   "In this moment of stillness, I find peace. My heart is calm, my mind is clear, my soul is balanced."

3. Enhancing Your Bathing Ritual

Incorporate additional elements to deepen your ritual:

- **Meditation:** Use the time in the bath to meditate on a specific intention or the themes of Yule.
- **Visualization:** Imagine the water glowing with golden light, cleansing and recharging your energy.
- **Offerings:** After your bath, pour some of the water outside as an offering to the Earth or spirits.

Practicing Self-Care to Stay Grounded during the Holidays

The holiday season can be overwhelming, with its demands on time, energy, and emotions. Self-care is essential for staying grounded and aligned with the spiritual essence of Yule.

1. Creating a Self-Care Routine

Develop a simple self-care routine to maintain balance:

- **Daily Rituals:** Start and end each day with small rituals, such as lighting a candle, journaling, or meditating.
- **Mindful Eating:** Choose nourishing, seasonal foods that support your body and spirit, such as root vegetables, spiced teas, and warming soups.
- **Rest and Recharge:** Prioritize rest, ensuring you have time to reflect and recharge amid the holiday rush.

2. Grounding Techniques

Grounding helps you stay connected to the present moment and aligned with your energy:

- **Breathing Exercises:** Practice deep breathing to calm your mind and center your energy.
- **Earthing:** Spend time outdoors, walking barefoot or sitting near trees to connect with the Earth's energy.
- **Grounding Stones:** Carry grounding crystals, such as hematite or black tourmaline, to stabilize your energy.

3. Managing Holiday Stress

Yule is a season of joy, but the holidays can also bring stress. Manage holiday overwhelm with these strategies:

- **Set Boundaries:** Protect your time and energy by saying no to activities that don't align with your priorities.
- **Simplify:** Focus on meaningful traditions rather than overloading yourself with obligations.
- **Ask for Support:** Reach out to friends, family, or a spiritual community if you need help or companionship.

4. Incorporating Yule Magic into Self-Care

Infuse your self-care practices with Yule's magical energy:

- **Gratitude Practice:** Each evening, reflect on three things you're grateful for, connecting with Yule's themes of abundance and renewal.
- **Seasonal Crafts:** Engage in creative activities, such as making ornaments or decorating with natural elements, to nurture your spirit.
- **Affirmations:** Use affirmations to reinforce your intentions, such as:
    - *"I am grounded and peaceful."*
    - *"I welcome renewal and light into my life."*

Sustaining Self-Care Beyond Yule

While Yule offers a special focus on renewal, self-care is a year-round necessity:

- **Create a Seasonal Cycle:** Align your self-care practices with the Wheel of the Year, adjusting them to the energy of each season.
- **Reflect and Reassess:** Regularly evaluate your needs and make changes to your routine as necessary.
- **Honor Your Limits:** Recognize when to rest and recharge, just as nature does during the winter months.

The Transformative Power of Ritual Baths and Self-Care

Ritual baths and self-care practices are powerful ways to connect with Yule's magic, allowing you to cleanse, renew, and stay grounded during the season. By dedicating time to nurture your body, mind, and spirit, you align with the Solstice's themes of light and transformation, ensuring you move into the new year with clarity and strength.

As you soak in the warmth of a ritual bath or take a moment to reflect by candlelight, remember that self-care is not just a luxury—it's a sacred act that honors your well-being and your connection to the cycles of nature. Let Yule inspire you to embrace the beauty of renewal, both in this season and throughout the year.

Chapter 25: Yule Reflections and Setting Intentions

Yule, the Winter Solstice, is a sacred time for introspection, renewal, and setting the stage for the year ahead. As the longest night gives way to the returning light, it symbolizes an opportunity to release the past and welcome new beginnings. By reflecting on the lessons of the past year and aligning with Yule's transformative energy, you can set powerful intentions that guide your spiritual and personal growth in the coming year.

This chapter explores rituals for reflecting on the past year, setting new intentions, and preparing your spirit for the New Year with the energy of Yule.

Rituals for Reflecting on the Past Year and Setting New Intentions

Reflection is a key aspect of Yule, allowing you to honor the experiences of the past year while creating space for new energy. Pairing reflection with intention-setting ensures a balanced approach to renewal.

1. Preparing for Reflection and Intention-Setting Rituals

Begin by creating a sacred space:

- **Cleanse Your Space:** Use incense, sage, or sound to clear stagnant energy.
- **Set the Mood:** Light candles, play soft music, and surround yourself with seasonal symbols like evergreens, holly, or Sun imagery.
- **Gather Materials:** Have a journal, pen, and any divination tools or ritual items you wish to use.

2. The Year in Review Ritual

This ritual helps you reflect on the past year with gratitude and understanding.

Materials Needed:

- A journal or blank paper.
- A white or gold candle.
- A small bowl of water or Earth for grounding.

Steps:

1. **Create Sacred Space:** Light the candle and sit quietly, focusing on your breath.
2. **Reflect on the Year:** Write down the significant events, emotions, and lessons of the past year. Consider:
   - What brought you joy or fulfillment?
   - What challenges did you overcome?
   - What lessons have you learned?
3. **Release and Honor:** If there are moments or energies you wish to release, write them on a separate piece of paper. Hold the paper over the candle flame (safely) and say:
   "I release what no longer serves me, with gratitude for the lessons it has taught me."
   Safely burn the paper or tear it into small pieces and bury it in the Earth.
4. **Close the Ritual:** Dip your fingers in the bowl of water or touch the Earth, grounding yourself in the present moment.

3. Setting New Intentions Ritual

This ritual focuses on aligning your energy with your goals for the coming year.

Materials Needed:

- A green or yellow candle (for growth and light).
- A piece of paper and pen.
- A small token (such as a crystal or charm) to represent your intention.

Steps:

1. **Focus on Your Intentions:** Sit quietly and think about what you want to manifest in the coming year. Reflect on:
    - Areas for personal growth.
    - Relationships or connections you want to nurture.
    - Goals for your career, health, or spiritual practice.
2. **Write Your Intentions:** Write each intention as a positive affirmation, such as:
    - *"I welcome abundance and joy into my life."*
    - *"I am resilient and open to growth."*
3. **Empower the Token:** Hold the token and visualize your intentions coming to fruition. Imagine the token glowing with energy.
4. **Light the Candle:** As you light the candle, say:
    "As the Sun returns, so too does my light. These intentions I plant, like seeds, to grow with the coming year."
5. **Close the Ritual:** Place the token on your altar or carry it with you as a reminder of your intentions.

Preparing Your Spirit for the New Year with Yule Energy

Yule's energy of renewal and transformation provides the perfect foundation for stepping into the New Year with clarity and purpose. By aligning your spirit with the light and hope of the Solstice, you ensure a strong start to the year ahead.

1. Aligning with the Returning Light

The Winter Solstice celebrates the rebirth of the Sun, symbolizing a time to bring light into your own life.

Daily Practices to Embrace Light:

- **Morning Candle Ritual:** Light a candle each morning and focus on a single word or theme for the day, such as "joy" or "abundance."
- **Affirmations:** Begin each day with affirmations that align with your intentions, such as:
  "I am guided by the light within me."
  "Each day brings new opportunities for growth."

2. Creating a Vision for the Year Ahead

Visualization helps you focus your energy and clarify your goals.

Steps for a Yule Visioning Ritual:

1. **Meditate on Your Goals:** Close your eyes and picture your ideal year unfolding. Imagine achieving your goals, feeling fulfilled, and experiencing joy.
2. **Create a Vision Board:** Gather images, words, and symbols that represent your intentions for the year. Arrange them on a board or page as a visual reminder of your goals.
3. **Seal with Gratitude:** Once your vision board is complete, place it near your altar or in a space where you'll see it regularly. Say:
   "With gratitude, I honor the light of Yule and the possibilities of the year to come."

3. Embracing Gratitude and Renewal

Gratitude amplifies the energy of renewal and sets a positive tone for the year ahead.

The Gratitude Jar Ritual:

- Find a jar or container and decorate it with Yule symbols.
- Each day, write down something you're grateful for and place it in the jar.
- At the next Yule, read through the notes to reflect on the abundance of the past year.

4. Grounding Practices for the New Year

Grounding ensures you stay balanced and focused as you step into the New Year.

Grounding Techniques:

- **Nature Walks:** Spend time outdoors, connecting with the Earth through mindful walking or tree meditation.
- **Crystals:** Carry grounding stones, such as hematite or black tourmaline, to stabilize your energy.
- **Breathing Exercises:** Practice deep, intentional breathing to center yourself in the present moment.

Sustaining Yule's Energy Beyond the Solstice

The magic of Yule doesn't end with the Solstice—it can guide you throughout the year:

- **Revisit Your Intentions:** Regularly reflect on the intentions you set during Yule, adjusting them as needed to stay aligned with your goals.
- **Honor the Seasons:** Connect with the energy of each season as part of the larger Wheel of the Year, maintaining a sense of renewal and balance.
- **Celebrate Small Wins:** Acknowledge progress and achievements, no matter how small, to keep your energy and motivation high.

The Transformative Power of Yule Reflections

Reflecting on the past year and setting intentions during Yule is a transformative practice that aligns you with the cycles of light and darkness. By embracing the energy of the Solstice, you release what no longer serves you, welcome new possibilities, and prepare your spirit for a year of growth and fulfillment.

As you carry Yule's lessons into the New Year, let the returning light inspire hope, strength, and clarity. Through mindful reflection and purposeful intention, you create a path that honors your journey and celebrates the magic of renewal.

Appendix A: Glossary of Yule Terms and Traditions

This glossary provides an extensive reference to the terms, symbols, and traditions associated with Yule, the Winter Solstice. It is designed to enhance your understanding of the season's rich cultural and spiritual significance, making it easier to incorporate these elements into your practice.

A

Altar: A sacred space used for rituals and ceremonies, often decorated with seasonal items like candles, evergreens, and symbols of the Sun during Yule.

Ancestors: Those who have come before us, often honored during Yule for their wisdom and guidance as the year transitions.

Amulet: A magical object or charm used for protection or to attract positive energy, often included in Yule gifts or rituals.

B

Bay Leaf: A herb often burned during Yule rituals to release old energy and set intentions for the coming year.

Balance: A key theme of Yule, representing the harmony between light and dark as the longest night of the year gives way to the return of the Sun.

Blessing Bowl: A bowl filled with symbolic items, such as herbs, crystals, or tokens, used to honor abundance and gratitude during Yule.

C

Candles: Central to Yule celebrations, candles symbolize the returning light of the Sun. Gold, white, green, and red candles are commonly used.

Cedar: A sacred evergreen associated with purification and protection, often used in Yule decorations and rituals.

Cleansing: A ritual act performed during Yule to clear away negative energy and make space for renewal, often involving incense, salt, or sound.

D

Divination: The practice of seeking insight or guidance through tools like tarot, runes, or pendulums, frequently performed during Yule to prepare for the year ahead.

Decorations: Items used to adorn homes, altars, or Yule trees, often including natural elements like pinecones, holly, and mistletoe.

E

Evergreens: Plants like pine, cedar, and fir that symbolize eternal life and resilience, central to Yule traditions and decorations.

Energy Work: Practices that focus on manipulating or balancing energy within and around the body, often included in Yule rituals for renewal and transformation.

F

Feast: A celebratory meal shared during Yule, featuring seasonal and symbolic foods like spiced cakes, roasted vegetables, and wassail.

Fire Rituals: Ceremonies involving candles, hearths, or bonfires, symbolizing warmth, transformation, and the returning light.

Frankincense: A resin burned as incense during Yule rituals to promote spiritual connection and clarity.

G

Gratitude: A core theme of Yule, focusing on reflecting on blessings and expressing thanks for the past year.

Greenery: Fresh or dried plants, such as holly, ivy, and pine, used to decorate and invoke the energy of nature during Yule.

Gifts: Offerings exchanged during Yule to symbolize generosity and the sharing of light and love.

H

Holly: A sacred plant associated with protection, balance, and the cycle of life, often used in Yule wreaths and decorations.

Hearth: The heart of the home, representing warmth, security, and community, often a focal point of Yule celebrations.

I

Incense: Aromatic materials burned during Yule rituals to cleanse energy and enhance the sacred atmosphere.

Intention: A focused desire or goal set during Yule, often through rituals or spells, to guide personal growth and transformation.

Ivy: A symbol of resilience and growth, often paired with holly in Yule decorations.

J

Journeying: A meditative or shamanic practice undertaken during Yule to explore the subconscious or connect with spiritual realms.

Joy: A central theme of Yule, reflecting the celebration of light, life, and the promise of renewal.

K

Kindling: Small twigs or wood used to start a Yule fire or burn a Yule log, symbolizing the spark of light returning to the world.

Kitchen Witchcraft: A practice that incorporates magical intentions into cooking and meal preparation, often emphasized during Yule feasts.

L

Light: A symbol of the Sun's return and a central theme of Yule, celebrated with candles, fires, and golden decorations.

Lavender: An herb used in Yule rituals for peace, calm, and balance, often included in ritual baths or sachets.

M

Mistletoe: A plant associated with fertility, love, and protection, often hung in doorways during Yule.

Meditation: A practice of focused stillness or visualization, often used during Yule for reflection and intention-setting.

Moon Phases: Though Yule focuses on the Sun, the Moon's cycles can also be honored, particularly if the Solstice coincides with a new or full Moon.

N

Nature Walk: A ritual activity during Yule to connect with the Earth, gather natural decorations, and honor the cycles of life.

New Year Intentions: Goals or desires set during Yule to align with the energies of renewal and growth.

O

Offerings: Gifts or tokens left for spirits, ancestors, or deities as part of Yule rituals, often including food, drink, or natural elements.

Ornaments: Decorations for Yule trees, often imbued with magical intent or representing personal and seasonal symbols.

P

Pendulum: A divination tool used during Yule for seeking guidance or answers to yes/no questions.

Protection Spells: Magical practices performed during Yule to guard against negativity and foster a sense of safety.

R

Renewal: A central theme of Yule, symbolizing the release of the old and the welcoming of new energy.

Ritual Bath: A sacred cleansing practice to align with the energy of Yule, often incorporating herbs, salts, and essential oils.

Runes: An ancient divination tool used during Yule to gain insights and set intentions for the year ahead.

S

Sun: The primary symbol of Yule, representing light, warmth, and the promise of renewal.

Sacred Space: A cleansed and consecrated area used for rituals, meditation, or reflection during Yule.

Seasonal Foods: Ingredients and dishes aligned with the themes of Yule, such as spiced cider, nuts, and dried fruits.

T

Tarot: A divination tool often used during Yule to explore themes of renewal, transformation, and the year ahead.

Traditions: Cultural or personal practices that celebrate Yule, including feasting, decorating, and exchanging gifts.

Transformation: A key aspect of Yule, symbolizing personal and spiritual growth as the light returns.

W

Wassail: A spiced drink associated with Yule feasting, often shared to promote good fortune and community spirit.

Wheel of the Year: The cyclical calendar of Sabbats, with Yule marking the turning point from darkness to light.

Wreath: A circular decoration made of evergreen branches, symbolizing the cycles of life and eternity.

Y

Yule: The Winter Solstice celebration, honoring the rebirth of the Sun and the promise of renewal and abundance.

Yule Log: A traditional wooden log burned during Yule rituals to symbolize the returning light and bring blessings for the year ahead.

Final Thoughts

This glossary serves as a foundational resource for understanding and integrating Yule's rich traditions into your practice. Whether you're new to Yule or deepening your existing connection to the season, these terms and their meanings illuminate the profound magic and symbolism of the Winter Solstice.

Message from the Author:

I hope you enjoyed this book, I love astrology and knew there was not a book such as this out on the shelf. I love metaphysical items as well. Please check out my other books:

-Life of Government Benefits

-My life of Hell

-My life with Hydrocephalus

-Red Sky

-World Domination:Woman's rule

-World Domination:Woman's Rule 2: The War

-Life and Banishment of Apophis: book 1

-The Kidney Friendly Diet

-The Ultimate Hemp Cookbook

-Creating a Dispensary(legally)

-Cleanliness throughout life: the importance of showering from childhood to adulthood.

-Strong Roots: The Risks of Overcoddling children

-Hemp Horoscopes: Cosmic Insights and Earthly Healing

- Celestial Hemp Navigating the Zodiac: Through the Green Cosmos

-Astrological Hemp: Aligning The Stars with Earth's Ancient Herb

-The Astrological Guide to Hemp: Stars, Signs, and Sacred Leaves

-Green Growth: Innovative Marketing Strategies for your Hemp Products and Dispensary

-Cosmic Cannabis

-Astrological Munchies

-Henry The Hemp

-Zodiacal Roots: The Astrological Soul Of Hemp

- Green Constellations: Intersection of Hemp and Zodiac

-Hemp in The Houses: An astrological Adventure Through The Cannabis Galaxy

-Galactic Ganja Guide

Heavenly Hemp

Zodiac Leaves

Doctor Who Astrology

Cannastrology

Stellar Satvias and Cosmic Indicas

<u>Celestial Cannabis: A Zodiac Journey</u>

AstroHerbology: The Sky and The Soil: Volume 1

AstroHerbology:Celestial Cannabis:Volume 2

Cosmic Cannabis Cultivation

The Starry Guide to Herbal Harmony: Volume 1

The Starry Guide to Herbal Harmony: Cannabis Universe: Volume 2

Yugioh Astrology: Astrological Guide to Deck, Duels and more

Nightmare Mansion: Echoes of The Abyss

Nightmare Mansion 2: Legacy of Shadows

Nightmare Mansion 3: Shadows of the Forgotten

Nightmare Mansion 4: Echoes of the Damned

The Life and Banishment of Apophis: Book 2

Nightmare Mansion: Halls of Despair

<u>Healing with Herb: Cannabis and Hydrocephalus</u>

<u>Planetary Pot: Aligning with Astrological Herbs: Volume 1</u>

Fast Track to Freedom: 30 Days to Financial Independence Using AI, Assets, and Agile Hustles

<u>Cosmic Hemp Pathways</u>

How to Become Financially Free in 30 Days: 10,000 Paths to Prosperity

Zodiacal Herbage: Astrological Insights: Volume 1

Nightmare Mansion: Whispers in the Walls

The Daleks Invade Atlantis

Henry the hemp and Hydrocephalus

10X The Kidney Friendly Diet
Cannabis Universe: Adult coloring book
Hemp Astrology: The Healing Power of the Stars
Zodiacal Herbage: Astrological Insights: Cannabis Universe: Volume 2
Planetary Pot: Aligning with Astrological Herbs: Cannabis Universes: Volume 2
Doctor Who Meets the Replicators and SG-1: The Ultimate Battle for Survival
Nightmare Mansion: Curse of the Blood Moon
The Celestial Stoner: A Guide to the Zodiac
Cosmic Pleasures: Sex Toy Astrology for Every Sign
Hydrocephalus Astrology: Navigating the Stars and Healing Waters
Lapis and the Mischievous Chocolate Bar

Celestial Positions: Sexual Astrology for Every Sign
Apophis's Shadow Work Journal: : A Journey of Self-Discovery and Healing
Kinky Cosmos: Sexual Kink Astrology for Every Sign
Digital Cosmos: The Astrological Digimon Compendium
Stellar Seeds: The Cosmic Guide to Growing with Astrology
Apophis's Daily Gratitude Journal

Cat Astrology: Feline Mysteries of the Cosmos
The Cosmic Kama Sutra: An Astrological Guide to Sexual Positions
Unleash Your Potential: A Guided Journal Powered by AI Insights
Whispers of the Enchanted Grove

Cosmic Pleasures: An Astrological Guide to Sexual Kinks

369, 12 Manifestation Journal

Whisper of the nocturne journal(blank journal for writing or drawing)

The Boogey Book

Locked In Reflection: A Chastity Journey Through Locktober

Generating Wealth Quickly:

How to Generate $100,000 in 24 Hours

Star Magic: Harness the Power of the Universe

The Flatulence Chronicles: A Fart Journal for Self-Discovery

The Doctor and The Death Moth

Seize the Day: A Personal Seizure Tracking Journal

The Ultimate Boogeyman Safari: A Journey into the Boogie World and Beyond

Whispers of Samhain: 1,000 Spells of Love, Luck, and Lunar Magic: Samhain Spell Book

Apophis's guides:

Witch's Spellbook Crafting Guide for Halloween

<u>Frost & Flame: The Enchanted Yule Grimoire of 1000 Winter Spells</u>

<u>The Ultimate Boogey Goo Guide & Spooky Activities for Halloween Fun</u>

Harmony of the Scales: A Libra's Spellcraft for Balance and Beauty

The Enchanted Advent: 36 Days of Christmas Wonders

Nightmare Mansion: The Labyrinth of Screams

Harvest of Enchantment: 1,000 Spells of Gratitude, Love, and Fortune for Thanksgiving

The Boogey Chronicles: A Journal of Nightly Encounters and Shadowy Secrets

The 12 Days of Financial Freedom: A Step-by-Step Christmas Countdown to Transform Your Finances

Sigil of the Eternal Spiral Blank Journal

A Christmas Feast: Timeless Recipes for Every Meal

Holiday Stress-Free Solutions: A Survival Guide to Thriving During the Festive Season

Yu-Gi-Oh! Holiday Gifting Mastery: The Ultimate Guide for Fans and Newcomers Alike

Holiday Harmony: A Hydrocephalus Survival Guide for the Festive Season

Celestial Craft: The Witch's Almanac for 2025 – A Cosmic Guide to Manifestations, Moons, and Mystical Events

Doctor Who: The Toymaker's Winter Wonderland

Tulsa King Unveiled: A Thrilling Guide to Stallone's Mafia Masterpiece

Pendulum Craft: A Complete Guide to Crafting and Using Personalized Divination Tools

Nightmare Mansion: Santa's Eternal Eve

Starlight Noel: A Cosmic Journey through Christmas Mysteries

The Dark Architect: Unlocking the Blueprint of Existence

Surviving the Embrace: The Ultimate Guide to Encounters with The Hugging Molly

The Enchanted Codex: Secrets of the Craft for Witches, Wiccans, and Pagans

Harvest of Gratitude: A Complete Thanksgiving Guide

Yuletide Essentials: A Complete Guide to an Authentic and Magical Christmas

Celestial Smokes: A Cosmic Guide to Cigars and Astrology

Living in Balance: A Comprehensive Survival Guide to Thriving with Diabetes Insipidus

Cosmic Symbiosis: The Venom Zodiac Chronicles

The Cursed Paw of Ambition

Cosmic Symbiosis: The Astrological Venom Journal

Celestial Wonders Unfold: A Stargazer's Guide to the Cosmos (2024-2029)

If you want solar for your home go here: https://www.harborso-lar.live/apophisenterprises/

Get Some Tarot cards: https://www.makeplayingcards.com/sell/apophis-occult-shop

Get some shirts: https://www.bonfire.com/store/apophis-shirt-emporium/

Instagrams:
@apophis_enterprises,
@apophisbookemporium,
@apophisscardshop
Twitter: @apophisenterpr1
Tiktok:@apophisenterprise
Youtube: @sg1fan23477, @FiresideRetreatKingdom
Hive: @sg1fan23477
CheeLee: @SG1fan23477

Podcast: Apophis Chat Zone: https://open.spotify.com/show/5zXbrCLEV2xzCp8ybrfHsk?si=fb4d4fdbdce44dec

Newsletter: https://apophiss-newsletter-27c897.beehiiv.com/

www.ingramcontent.com/pod-product-compliance
Lightning Source LLC
Chambersburg PA
CBHW071745150726
47998CB00005B/1811